THE NEW CUCINA
ITALIANA

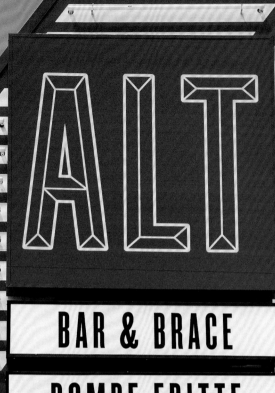

ALT

BAR & BRACE

BOMBE FRITTE

DOLCI · BISCOTTI

POLLO FRITTO

PANE · FOCACCE

STAZIONE
del GUSTO

THE NEW CUCINA ITALIANA

**What to Eat, What to Cook
& Who to Know in Italian Cuisine Today**

Laura Lazzaroni
Photographs by Alberto Blasetti

RIZZOLI
NEW YORK

New York · Paris · London · Milan

The beginning   6
What we talk about when we talk about the "New Cucina Italiana"   9
How to use this book   16
Pantry and techniques   17

CHAPTER 1: MENTORS

Niko Romito, Reale (Abruzzo)   **22**
Recipes 34
Paolo Lopriore, Il Portico (Lombardia)   **44**
Recipes 50

CHAPTER 2: FARMERS & FORAGERS

Juri Chiotti, Reis Cibo Libero di Montagna (Piemonte)   **56**
Recipes 60
Alice Delcourt, Erba Brusca (Lombardia)   **64**
Recipes 70
Luca Grasselli, Cascina Lagoscuro (Lombardia)   **72**
Recipes 78
Damiano Donati, Fuoco e Materia (Toscana)   **82**
Recipes 88
Alessandro Miocchi & Giuseppe Lo Iudice, Retrobottega (Lazio)   **92**
Recipes 98
Francesco & Vincenzo Montaruli, Mezza Pagnotta (Puglia)   **102**
Recipes 108

CHAPTER 3: SUNDAY RESTAURATEURS

Gianluca Gorini, DaGorini (Emilia-Romagna)   **112**
Recipes 120
Benedetto Rullo, Lorenzo Stefanini, Stefano Terigi, Ristorante Giglio (Toscana)   **124**
Recipes 132
Riccardo Camanini, Lido 84 (Lombardia)   **134**
Recipes 140

CHAPTER 4: FINE DINING CREATIVES

Antonia Klugmann, L'Argine a Vencò (Friuli-Venezia Giulia)   **144**
Recipes 152
Davide Caranchini, Materia (Lombardia)   **156**
Recipes 162
Gianni Dezio, Tosto (Abruzzo)   **164**
Recipes 168
Isabella Potì & Floriano Pellegrino, Bros' (Puglia)   **170**
Recipes 176

CHAPTER 5: PIZZAIOLI

Franco Pepe, Pepe in Grani (Campania)   **182**
Recipes 188
Ciro Oliva, Concettina ai Tre Santi (Campania)   **190**
Recipes 194

CHAPTER 6: FORCES OF NEO-OSTERIE & NEO-TRATTORIE

Diego Rossi, Trippa (Lombardia)   **198**
Recipes 204
Francesco Capuzzo Dolcetta, Marzapane (Lazio)   **206**
Recipes 212
Stefano & Mattia Manias, Al Cjasal (Veneto)   **216**
Recipes 220
Lorenzo Costa & Daniele Bendanti, Oltre (Emilia-Romagna)   **222**
Recipes 226
Pietro Vergano & Andrea Gherra, Consorzio/Banco (Piemonte)   **228**
Recipes 234
The Fooders, Mazzo (Lazio)   **238**
Recipes 242
Martina Miccione & Carla De Girolamo, Tipografia Alimentare (Lombardia)   **244**
Recipes 248

Finale   250
Restaurant Directory   252

THE BEGINNING

I'm standing in the middle of Interstate 17, on the Piana delle Cinque Miglia—the Five Mile Plateau—near the border between Abruzzo and Molise. Alberto Blasetti is lying on the road in front of me, camera in hand, trying to capture the vastness of this expanse. Except for this narrow strip of asphalt, empty as far as the eye can see, we're surrounded by nothing but nature. Abruzzo, an unspoiled gem at the center of Italy, is full of plateaus like this. Winds sucker-punch you here, and winters can be brutal—around us is Italy's second largest ski area—but starting in spring the *altopiani* wear triumphant blankets of mountain flowers and maturing mountain wheat while sheep and cows graze, placid.

I'm here to meet with Niko Romito, one of Italy's most inspiring chefs, the champion of a new league of extraordinary restaurateurs who are shaping the movement of a "new cucina italiana." It's the first stop of a road trip that will take me through my homeland, running the gamut of gritty and glamorous, comfort and research, metropolitan and rural, punk and spiritual. From Piedmont to Puglia, I will visit a couple dozen restaurants, give or take—casual joints, fine dining institutions, and some places that elude categorization.

As I stand on the Cinque Miglia, I think about what brought me here. I embarked on this journey to answer a disarmingly simple question: what do we talk about when we talk about cucina italiana today? We have learned so much from our *nonne* but we've also severed that umbilical cord. Our *trattorie* are evolving and our fine dining is so much more than tweezers and flower petals. There's a quiet revolution happening. But what exactly is the "new cucina italiana"? Who are the women and men shaping it? What do food enthusiasts all over the world need to know before they come here to Instagram the umpteenth plate of amatriciana? (Not that there's nothing wrong with amatriciana, heaven knows.)

I have a problem with a particular misconception surrounding Italian cuisine. There is a tendency to reduce it to one of two things: stereotypical traditional fare, like cacio e pepe, tortellini, and fritto misto or avant-garde, hyper conceptualized dishes. With the former, the dishes that have made Italy's fortune for their alluring simplicity, flavor, and comfort have also trapped it in a never-ending cycle of reiterated clichés. The latter is rarely appealing to non-gourmets (deconstructed carbonara, anyone?). These two approaches are far from dead, but there is also something else, something more.

I'm a home cook, a bread-baker, and I have been writing professionally about food for the best part of my life. I know many chefs in this movement, I've had lengthy post-meal discussions with them about their dishes, sitting in the heat of their kitchens; I've talked to other journalists, academics, producers; I've seen these chefs come together as a collective, moving past their individualistic ways towards a more collaborative endeavor; I've watched them find a voice, have fun, and be free: I figured this was a story worth telling. There are plenty of recipes for those who want to bring the flavors of the new cucina italiana into their home kitchens, wherever those may be.

As I'm thinking all this, a carabinieri jeep slowly approaches us. We know we've been lucky, not a car or truck driving by, otherwise this stop on the Interstate could have proven to be very dangerous. The carabinieri seem to think so too: as they pass us, one of them rolls down the window, shoots me one lingering look of disapproval and says, with a slight Abruzzese accent: *"Volete morire per una foto?"*: is a good shot worth dying for?

Little did I know that within a year from that close encounter with the Italian law enforcement the world would be hit by a pandemic that would jeopardize the survival of its population — and of all businesses, including (perhaps particularly) restaurants.

As I revisit these first lines I burn with an even more tenacious passion for the cooking women and men of my country, having witnessed how hard they fought and how ingeniously they worked to stay afloat amidst the turbulence (with little help from the institutions).

While I wrap the book up they're getting ready to reopen. And while it's too early to tell what the actual toll of the COVID-19 emergency on the industry will be, I know their determination to resume caring for their customers and the legacy of their flavors are strong and will carry on.

So come travel with me.
What a trip.

Castel di Sangro, May 2019–Milan, May 2020

WHAT WE TALK

ABOUT

WHEN WE TALK

ABOUT THE

"NEW CUCINA ITALIANA"

SLIPPERY LITTLE SUCKER (The impossibility of defining la cucina italiana)

"Of course, you know there is one major obstacle you'll have to overcome while working on your book." I'm talking with my good friend Marco Bolasco, one of Italy's most respected food critics and director of nonfiction at Giunti Editore, and he's trying to reassure me, so to speak. I look worried, he looks amused. "The problem, as you know, is that when all is said and done it's impossible to define Italian cuisine."

He's not wrong. It's hard to define something as multi-layered and multi-faceted as our gastronomy. It's a slippery little sucker (yes, I'm quoting *Pretty Woman*). Our country has always been at the intersection of great fluxes—of peoples, cultures, and ingredients; as a result, our cuisine has absorbed so many different influences it's hard to keep track. The way we eat has been shaped by the Roman Empire, the Middle Ages, the Renaissance, and nineteenth-century France (think of Carême and Escoffier), as much as by the Industrial Revolution, the Great Wars, and the fifties. Socially, our references have been the cultivated menus of the aristocracy and the clergy, the poor man's table, and in more recent times the dietary schizophrenia (canned food meets health food) of the mainstream.

We've gone from a cuisine of spices and artifice (such was the spirit of ancient Rome, the Middle Ages and the Renaissance) to an ingredient-centric cuisine and over the course of it all we've ping-ponged from a polyphony of regional voices to a somewhat unified identity and back to territorial fragmentation. It's a lot to digest. How do you summarize all this in one definition?

But even if it's impossible to come up with one perfect definition for la cucina italiana, there are some indisputable identifying elements everyone should learn to recognize. "First, the whole body of Italian recipes is based on the rich biodiversity of our habitat," says Marco. "The identity of the products we use in the kitchen is the driving force. It's a cuisine of the ingredient, as opposed to a cuisine defined by technique, like modern Spanish cooking, for instance." This doesn't mean Italian cuisine is not technical, it's just understanding what comes first.

"Secondly, it's a Mediterranean cuisine. When you think of an Italian dish you think of *spaghetti al pomodoro*, which comes from Naples, and when you think of products you think of vegetables and extra-virgin olive oil, which are typical of Italy's center and south."

There is also a third defining element, and that is the experience of our cuisine. The way we approach the table is convivial, warm, familiar. Cooking and eating are forms of entertainment, and they're supposed to make people feel good. Marco points out that no restaurateur can afford to forget this, no matter how high up the ladder she or he is. "This is why Niko Romito serves an elevated version of *pane e prosciutto* in his three-Michelin-star restaurant and why a cerebral chef like Paolo Lopriore has abandoned fine dining to explore a format based on shared plates."

THE TORTELLINO FACTOR

Then there's the question of the tortellino. The emancipation that has proven to be crucial for the development of a "new" cucina italiana started when we realized we had to dial down our romanticism and outgrow the very same nonne we kept referencing like our lives depended on it. This mind switch has nothing to do with being cynical: it's about finally realizing that our grandmothers were not infallible and there are things they did that can be improved upon. (If these concepts sound familiar, by the way, it's because Massimo Bottura has been broadcasting them to the world for two decades.)

It's true that very few chefs can roll a paper-thin layer of fresh pasta like a sfoglina, but this has to do with a legacy of ritualistic gestures, safely locked in our elders' hands, not necessarily with formalized cooking techniques: not all nonne mastered these and because the science of food hadn't been popularized yet when they took to the stoves, they weren't familiar with how to best transform ingredients without compromising their nutritional values and structures while still obtaining the most delicious results. (Because of this, they sometimes tended to go heavy with the condiments.)

Chefs these days have a deeper understanding of both how ingredients are physically transformed to become dishes and how they are metabolized in our bodies, and they have references available to them that transcend tradition. Their grandmothers (or great-grandmothers, or mothers: depending on their age, the generation they refer to changes) serve as inspiration for one fundamental element: flavor. While the young stars of our cuisine are contemporary in their methods, experiences, and ideas, they all mention a sixth sense for "absolute" Italian flavor which they say can't be learned, but only absorbed through exposure. This is the foundation.

"Kill the nonne" might sound a bit harsh, but this is the idea: for the people shaping our new cuisine, tradition is something one must know and absorb at such a deep, cellular level that it can then be forgotten. These new chefs are not covering old songs, they are trying to write original music that people still connect with.

THE MAESTRO FACTOR

There is another level of emancipation our chefs are experiencing, and that involves the lesson of the maestri. A quick recap of our culinary history should come handy at this point.

It is a truth universally acknowledged that France has been a driving force for the development of virtually all Western cuisine and Italy is no exception. The latest Italian maestro to draw from the lesson of the French was Gualtiero Marchesi: many important chefs, like Paolo Lopriore, Carlo Cracco, Davide Oldani, Andrea Berton, and Enrico Crippa are disciples of his, so there is lineage and through that lineage that French-inspired approach went on.

The peak of Marchesi's influence was in the 1980s. Then came the '90s and Spain's Ferran Adrià and El Bulli detonated in the culinary world like a hand grenade. Before closing his restaurant in 2011 this Catalan powerhouse created an immense body of work and with his unbridled creativity he gave the culinary community the ultimate gift: freedom. Other chefs across Europe and the world were galvanized: all of a sudden, experimenting in the kitchen seemed doable, necessary. I dare you to find a chef who hasn't tried to reproduce Adrià's olive spherification.

But that kind of momentum is destined to fade, and not many geniuses are born in a given decade: eventually the collective high was followed by a comedown. Globalization eventually spurred a distaste for the avant-garde, and in a classic pendulum shift, an affirmation of cultural identity and introspection arose. In Italy, chefs felt a sudden longing for a return to simpler, more authentic things. While they couldn't forget the lessons they had learned from Adrià (the importance of research, new culinary formats, and fun), they started rediscovering figures like Valeria Piccini and Fulvio Pierangelini who, in their Tuscan restaurants (Caino, in Montemerano, and the legendary Gambero Rosso, in San Vincenzo), had written pages of spontaneous, poetic cuisine, simple, cultivated, and delicious.

Chefs are still going to France and Spain. Some go to Asia, South America, and Northern Europe (the France of the culinary years 2000s). Some actually never leave Italy. Some have traditional culinary school training, some never serve under a particular maestro for more than a few weeks. Someone takes the road less traveled, someone takes the high road. All these roads lead back here.

TRADITION VS. LOCAVORISM

Up until a century ago, travel wasn't something everybody could do and this created boundaries around culinary traditions. With no Google or email or Instagram, exchange of ideas and recipes with distant parts of the country wasn't easy. Sure, there were books, but even those had a modest and limited distribution as compared to today.

Many chefs, especially the young, now feel a spontaneous calling for the things of their territory, products especially. It's a way to reconnect to an identity they were somehow already aware of, instinctively. It has to do with a place, with local supply chains, for instance, not so much with a desire to be "regional"; it's even more circumscribed than that. Maybe it has something to do also with what they learned (or re-learned, rather) from Northern Europe: the desire to work with the people who surround them by choice, not necessity. This doesn't mean they're being "traditional." Many of these "locavore chefs" are in fact very contemporary in their approach to cuisine.

Yet not all chefs identify with a specific place or region. Some feel the need to embrace a more "universal" Italian canon that wraps everything in its arms and goes beyond a sense of place. And this is true for the ingredients they use too: we are fortunate enough to live in an era where quality control is high enough to allow, say, Lombardic chefs to map the way their lambs are raised, even if they come from Sicily. As I was researching this book I asked all chefs this specific question, whether they felt Italian or local first. The group is almost equally split. It's an interesting thing to keep in mind when judging the new cucina italiana as a whole.

NEW FINE DINING, NEO-TRATTORIA, AND THE RISTORANTE CLASSICO

We've talked about the food, but what about the places where this food is consumed?

For the longest time restaurants in Italy have fallen under one of two categories: the *"ristorante familiare"* or "trattoria"; and the French-style, grand restaurant (of which the hotel restaurant, catering mainly to tourists, represented an offshoot). At some point during the past few years we started wondering whether it'd be possible to develop a new model. It had been done elsewhere: a good example is Spain, where Adrià revolutionized the tasting menu canon by cross-pollinating it with the tapas bar experience.

At a fine dining level, Italy has witnessed quite a lot of inventiveness: as a format the *"ristorante gastronomico"* is freer creatively, naturally bolder. The demographics of the public it caters to allow for a greater degree of risk-taking.

But what we really need to innovate is the trattoria. First, because this is "our" trademark, probably the most readily identifiable as Italian. Secondly, because it speaks to more people, its language being more universal: a new trattoria format would have more impact than a new kind of fine dining might. As Carlo Petrini says, gastronomy is interesting when it's complex, holistic, widespread. This resonates even louder in a country like Italy, where fantastic things can be done with just bread and prosciutto.

But it's not easy to rethink the trattoria, to unglue it from the past, from its quasi-folkloristic heritage. It needs an injection of fresh energy, similar to what has happened in the wine world, with a new generation going back to the vineyard and taking over the craft of their fathers and grandfathers. It has to define itself through its food as much as through its atmosphere, the clientele, and the role it serves, so these elements need to step into the present too.

There's another genre, born in the cities out of the economic boom of the fifties (historically more recent than the trattoria and the fine dining restaurant), which I feel represents Italy well and probably needs work to be brought into the contemporary: it's the "bourgeoise" restaurant, the classic restaurant with a combination of familiar fare and classic service. A nice risotto served by a waiter in a vest and bow-tie. A self-serve buffet of antipasti and a nicely stocked cellar. Not fine dining, not quite trattoria either (and just like the latter, more about service and atmosphere than food).

When we talk about "new cucina italiana" we mean all registers of the dining experience. If fine dining restaurants are the Ferraris of food, elite places where big bucks can be spent on research, ingredients, and carefully engineered protocols, the trattoria is where we re-educate the masses. In this book you'll find both, and also many things in between. We need it all, the high and the low: they're stronger when they work together.

"NEW"

AT HOME

HOW TO USE THIS BOOK

I've long had a desire to show the world the cucina italiana I get to experience and love, every single day. I felt the world had a somewhat incorrect idea of its true character, and with the confidence typical of a much younger age than mine, I thought "I can fix that!" Ha! I ended up writing an atypical book, which means there's more than one way to put it to good use.

You can definitely use it as a cookbook.
In the following pages you will find recipes from the restaurants I visited during my "grand tour" of Italy. They are organized by restaurant, and grouped by category of cuisine and format (fine dining, new trattoria, etc.). You will find a mix of first courses, second courses, and desserts. There will be pizza and bread. You will also find quite a few antipasti and *contorni* (sides), both being unique staples of the Italian meal, and by "meal" I mean the quasi-religious, ritualistic service that allows the antipasto and contorno the full dignity of a proper course. Keep in mind that depending on the type of restaurant they come from, servings will be more or less abundant.

I know our job was much easier than it would have been had I written this only ten years ago: I lived in New York from 2003 to 2008 and I remember how difficult it was in my early days there to find more than a couple generic brands of rigatoni. Quality pasta as well as many other original Italian ingredients are now more readily available in the U.S. You should be able to find all ingredients (or valid substitutes) at your local supermarket or specialty store.

All recipes have also been adapted to make them replicable in a non-professional environment, without the equipment and labor force of a proper restaurant kitchen. Simplicity is key to Italian cuisine, but a restaurant is a restaurant. We tried to maintain the flavor, texture, and aesthetics of each dish, but most importantly, we sought to preserve their spirit. We asked chefs to provide us with tricks to pass on to you because the core of all Italian cuisine comes from a tradition of home cooking ("know it to forget it," remember?), and all chefs were happy to oblige and had quite a few great tips to share.

I hope you will cook out of this book, and that while you wait for your dish to be ready and you flip through these pages—maybe dipping a chunk of Niko Romito's bread (recipe on page 38) in the sauce for Ristorante Giglio's Minestra di Triglie, Miso e Shiso (Red mullet, Miso and Shiso soup, recipe on page 133), possibly sipping on a glass of wine, or a very dry Martini, or an Amaro Centerba (sorry, I don't do spritzes)—you'll feel transported here.

You definitely don't have to use it as a cookbook.
If you're one of those people who buy cookbooks to read the text and look at the photos, well, I hope you will approach this as you would a coming-of-age novel: I hope you will find my adventures on the road entertaining, and the stories of these women, men, products, and places inspiring.

You could also use this as a guidebook, connecting the dots of these restaurants, north to south. I like picturing my imaginary readers sitting cross-legged on the floor, drafting and sharing itineraries from, say, Veneto to Abruzzo. Many of the regions I have visited are little-known even to Italians, and the idea of opening these treasure chests to your careful explorations fills me with joy.

Whether you cook or just follow along my journey, I hope you will feel the irresistible urge to come to Italy in person and taste it for yourself. Autostrade per l'Italia, the company that runs and maintains our highways, recently launched a beautiful ad campaign. The tagline reads: *Sei in un paese meraviglioso* (You're in a gorgeous country).

PANTRY AND TECHNIQUES

While the level of difficulty varies from recipe to recipe, I believe you will find most of this book's dishes to be very approachable. However, I recommend you read over each recipe carefully before your first attempt, and that you familiarize yourself with the following tips on ingredients and special equipment.

Salt. Italians are still relatively indifferent to the widespread use of different kinds of salt in commercial and home kitchens, opting instead for regular sea salt: we suggest you use that for all recipes. Should you want to substitute with kosher, just keep in mind you will have to increase the amount to your preference.

Pepper. If not otherwise specified, we recommend using freshly ground black pepper.

Olive oil. Even the most basic recipe calling for olive oil relies on the quality of the product: choose extra-virgin olive oil, cold-pressed, preferably Italian, and unless specified, opt for a mild tasting variety.

Frying oil. Because olive oil is very flavorful, the majority of chefs use less pungent oils with high smoke points, like sunflower seed oil, or other vegetable oils, for frying.

Grapeseed oil. This should be the choice when making mayonnaise or when preparing flavored oils: its neutral flavor won't overpower other ingredients.

Butter. In any Italian kitchen, whether domestic or commercial, butter is almost always unsalted.

Capers. Salt-packed capers are preferable because they maintain their flavor and texture better than the vinegar-packed variety. Remember you'll have to soak them in fresh water and rinse several times before using.

Anchovies. You can either use salt-packed or oil-packed anchovies. When opting for the latter, remember to save the oil, which is infused with exceptional umami notes and can be used to create a substitute for *colatura di alici*, our beloved fish sauce.

Pasta. Not all brands of dry pasta are equal: elements such as the quality of wheat and its milling, the water used, the extrusion and drying, all contribute to the final texture and flavor, carrying over to the dish. Though most chefs swear by specific brands, we chose not to mention any by name (the same goes for rice and flours). We do, however, recommend you buy high quality Italian durum wheat dry pasta. Shapes are always specified and should not be substituted. Pasta should always be cooked al dente (for less time than indicated on the package), in boiling, salted water. Salt should be added when the water is already boiling, before you add the pasta.

Rice. Italians use different varieties of rice for different purposes, depending on the size of the grain, the amount of starch released during cooking, and the desired final texture. In this book you'll find recipes that call for three main varieties: Arborio, Carnaroli (best suited for risotto), and Roma (best for *minestre* and *timballi*, or molded rice casseroles).

Flours. Italian flours are very different from those available in the U.S. Granularity varies, as does protein content and gluten strength. We have four types of bread flour (00, 0, 1, and 2), based on protein content and on how much bran is sifted from the flour after milling (2 being the closest to whole-wheat). Italians also use a lot of durum wheat flour, for pasta and (particularly in the center and south) bread: it's sold as *semolato*, *semola*, *semola rimacinata* (from coarser to finer). Italians also use quite a few old varieties of wheat flours, which are not easily available in the U.S. We tested all pizza and bread recipes with U.S. flours. Because we found commercial U.S. bread flours to have a stronger gluten than Italian flours (yielding "tighter" doughs than we wanted) we opted for unbleached all-purpose flour as base flour. One of our bread recipes (Sourdough Bread with Potatoes, on page 38) called for type 0 flour, so in order to come as close to that as possible, we used a blend of unbleached all-purpose and stoneground white whole-wheat all-purpose flours. In addition, the recipe called for some semola rimacinata: while some U.S. stores will carry that, you can also replace it with durum semolina. We recommend you always buy organic flours.

Starter. You can either make your sourdough starter, or ask your local sourdough bakery for a small amount and build on that with multiple feedings. Remember the texture you're looking for is creamy, so a stiff starter won't do. If you want to attempt to make your own, the recipe is on page 39. Care for your starter and it will serve you well.

Yeast. Though Italians often use fresh yeast, we substituted active dry yeast for your convenience.

Offal. A few recipes in this book call for the use of offal and other animal parts that are most often discarded in the U.S. The Italian snout-to-tail movement is not just a trend, but a long-standing tradition borne out of the need to use every part of the animal: we encourage you to stretch the limits of your palate and try something you wouldn't normally eat. Make sure you procure these pieces from a trusted butcher with high-quality meat.

Cross-referencing recipes. Many of the recipes in this book are designed to use scraps or leftover bits from other recipes, so be on the lookout for notes featuring waste-saving cross-references.

Special equipment. For the fresh pasta recipes, a pasta maker is a time-saver, but not indispensable. A fine mesh sieve and cheesecloth are pretty fundamental for filtering and you'll find them mentioned often. We recommend always keeping an instant read thermometer at hand and using a Dutch oven for your Sourdough Bread with Potatoes recipe. You will find notes for these and other special tools whenever necessary.

NIKO ROMITO
PAOLO LOPRIORE

MENTORS

NIKO

ROMITO

As soon as we whistle and call their names, the two white spots on the side of the mountain stop. Even if I can't really see them, I can imagine a pair of leonine heads raised in the crisp air, their ears perked up. They're past the vineyard and the first fuzz of woods, where wolves and bears sometimes descend roaming for food. They're not scared of those. "Pane! Olio!" we call again, and the two Abruzzese shepherds start coming down as fast as hockey pucks on ice, their silhouettes bigger by the second, their charge steadfast. I brace myself for the impact.

These guardians of Casadonna have fur of the same color as the stones that make up this sixteenth-century former monastery in Castel di Sangro, serving as headquarters of Niko Romito's operations: his three-Michelin-star restaurant, Reale, is here, as are the nine rooms reserved for his guests, and Accademia Niko Romito, his private institute for culinary education. Who would have thought that what was once a heap of broken walls (stripped even of the Virgin Mary statue that used to protect them), overlooking an ancient transhumance route on the fringes of the Parco Nazionale d'Abruzzo, would be turned into one of the most legendary gastronomical destinations in the country?

Back when Romito first drove past these ruins, Reale had two Michelin stars and occupied the former location of his family trattoria, in the small ski town of Rivisondoli, a few kilometers away. Seeing what was left of the monastery, the young chef recognized his ticket to the third star. He didn't have the means to buy the six hectare property but that didn't discourage him. He went to his mother, told her "You've got

to have faith," got some money from the family, negotiated a crazy double life-long mortgage, and bought Casadonna.

It takes special foresight to see the arc connecting potential and fulfillment. Romito has it. He sees what things could become. "If I hadn't become a cook I would have been a builder," he often says, expressing his love for striking materials and ingenious architectural solutions, which Casadonna is full of. The interior walls are made of slaked lime paste, polished with wax and a woolen cloth, an old technique Romito himself showed his construction workers. There's reclaimed wood, antique flagstones, and ceramic tiles: they weren't trendy when he first chose them.

The restored monastery is like a populated version of Superman's Fortress of Solitude, the one place on Earth where the Abruzzese chef feels safe, grounded, where he fully recharges. It's also the secret behind his singular genius: it protects him from the bullshit of the industry, and from unnecessary influences. Part of his strength comes precisely from having controlled such influences: he's self-taught, save for a few culinary courses and a short stint under Valeria Piccini. "I'm like a sponge, I absorb everything," he said when I first met him. Then, he would laugh a nervous laugh and say *Oh, Madonnina* (the equivalent of "Oh, Lordy") a lot, his eyes big and wide. He rarely spoke English, even though his mother Giovanna, who is an English teacher (with an infallible recipe for *ciambellone*, a traditional bundt cake), spoke it to him when he was little. Perhaps it had something to do with being the youngest, and the only boy, of four children. Twin sisters Cristiana and

Sabrina, and Debora, the eldest, are a force to be reckoned with. Cristiana is Casadonna's general manager and the director of Reale's dining room; Sabrina oversees the front of house in one of the group's other restaurants, in Rome; Debora, a banking executive, is Niko's confidant, the only one who can keep up when he starts talking bottom lines.

Romito and his sisters were born in Abruzzo and studied in Rome, while their father was setting up Reale, first as a pastry and coffee shop, then as a trattoria. When he fell ill, Niko, who was in his mid-twenties at the time, and Cristiana went back to Rivisondoli to run it. Niko didn't know anything about cooking (but had dropped out of business school a few exams short of graduating, and tried his hand at selling Balinese furniture), and Cristiana (who had studied to be an interpreter and dreamed of being a flight attendant) didn't drink alcohol. Even though the relationship with his father had been difficult (Romito's hero was his mother's father, his "nonnò"), after his death he decided he'd sacrifice the perspective of a normal, quieter life to carry on what he had built. Cristiana became a sommelier, and along the way Niko discovered he was ambitious. In seven years they went from zero to three Michelin stars and garnered so many other accolades that I've lost count.

When people ask me who the best chef in Italy is, I dodge the question. "Best" is a complex notion, one with too many variables. But there is one chef who I believe represents the future of our cuisine, an "absolute" chef who combines superior gastronomic sensibility, astute entrepreneurial vision, and an uncanny ability to transfer his knowledge to the public and young chefs hungry for inspiration: Romito. While not every chef is born with a desire to communicate concepts (not everyone must), those who do rarely move past a basic narrative. Finding new words, casting a new vocabulary to tell the story of your dishes is the first step. Then comes writing a new grammar and ultimately a new language. A few manage to get to the first step. Romito mastered the second. He doesn't do it just because he is generous. He started codifying his cuisine (namely with the manifesto *10 Lezioni di Cucina*, which we co-wrote in 2014) for the same reason why he standardizes his processes: because he cares about recognition, the paternity of his ideas, and because codifying and standardizing allow him to dream big; he can grow, knowing his legacy is protected even if he can't be hands-on for everything.

Romito has projects covering the whole spectrum of food, from luxurious to fast casual. In all of them, the experience of food is as central as food itself, and the food is quintessentially Italian. On the high end there is Reale and also Il Ristorante Niko Romito, a compendium of Italian gastronomic archetypes (the definitive antipasto all'italiana, lasagna, veal Milanese, etc.) he designed for Bulgari Hotels & Resorts in Beijing, Shanghai, Dubai, Milan, and Paris. At the opposite end of the spectrum there is Alt, which combines the functions of a diner (it's on the interstate that crosses Abruzzo close to Casadonna, connecting Italy's east and west coasts) and the heart of a neo-trattoria. There's also Intelligenza Nutrizionale, the scientific protocol he developed with Rome's Università La Sapienza, revolutionizing hospital catering (with potential applications in all cafeteria settings). In between the two ends there's Spazio, a contemporary riff on the concept of an everyday restaurant, impeccable and affordable, the missing link between neo-trattoria and fine dining (with locations in Milan and Rivisondoli), and Spazio Bar e Cucina, in Rome, combining a little bit of Alt and Spazio. Gruppo Niko Romito alone (not counting Bulgari) employs 130 people. What's really impressive is how coherent the whole system is. One thread connects everything. Most ideas and dishes are developed at Reale and then trickle down to other projects. Sometimes the ideation process moves bottom up. A textbook product cycle if you're talking about design or fashion, less so in gastronomy.

A prime example of what Romito calls *cucina circolare* (circular cuisine) is his cauliflower (recipe on page 37). "At Reale we steam it, then let it mature for three days, and finally serve it on top of a paste of cauliflower, mustard, and vinegar, glazing it with cauliflower reduction. Elements of this dish have found their way also to a pasta course we serve at Bulgari and to one of Spazio's appetizers." The almost compulsive layering of the same ingredient is one of Romito's signature moves, the result of a sophisticated grasp of culinary techniques, from the most fundamental to the most advanced, and of a profound knowledge of the ingredient itself, along with a natural aversion to anything superfluous. It leads to dishes that are at once deceptively simple, incredibly flavorful, astonishingly light: a powerful trifecta many have tried (and failed) to copy.

There are more examples like this. One of the most popular dishes on Bulgari's menu is veal Milanese: Spazio has its own version of it, In Carpione (recipe on page 43), as does Alt. "I like when I can feed off the base of the pyramid, when I have to solve problems for the collective and then carry the solutions up to the top. It happened, for instance, when I had to find a new way to make sauces for the hospital: they had to be inexpensive, fat free, tasty, and easy to handle by unskilled personnel." The answer to that problem was "osmotic contamination": by combining water and ingredients in a sous-vide pouch, flavor is transferred and fixed. It costs very little, it's healthy, and once the protocol is standardized, anyone can replicate it. "We made a delicious pasta sauce with tomatoes, olives, capers, garlic, and vinegar, a very Italian combination of flavors: it ended up in a salt cod dish at Alt. We used the same technique to create the smoky duck water we

serve alongside our cold duck course at Reale. It's a very clean dish, fat free, and when you bite into it you get an explosion of so many different notes."

Reale's dishes can be very comforting; they also feel invariably familiar, something one wouldn't necessarily expect from fine dining. There is no question all of Romito's cuisine transcends regionality: certain ingredients (legumes, lamb, saffron, truffles) and specific preparations (such as the Assoluto di Cipolla, recipe on page 35) are unequivocally territorial, but the underlying philosophy serves as a blueprint for contemporary Italian dining.

Just in his mid-forties, Romito has been able to craft definitive versions of our most culturally significant courses: broth, soup, dry pasta, fresh pasta, meat. His vegetable-only dishes (which, in keeping with his cucina circolare concept, are adapted and served in all his restaurant formats, see recipes on pages 37 and 41) are as satisfying as steaks. Reale's bread (recipe on page 38) is arguably the best restaurant bread in Italy, and is served as its own course. His research on local heritage wheat and doughs has spurred yet another project, Pane. In a state-of-the-art facility adjoining Alt, Romito's bakers produce seven hundred kilos of loaves every day (in addition to viennoiserie, cookies, cakes, and the fried Bomba still made following his father's recipe, a doughnut so good and light it's life-altering), supplying Alt, Spazio, and Bulgari Milano, and recently even a test group of supermarkets in Abruzzo.

"Come taste this." Niko is standing by Reale's pass, his back against the wall. This is where you'll find him ninety percent of the time: he even takes to the tiles behind him to write inspirational (or cautionary) quotes for himself. One says *"Mai una gioia,"* (never a joy)—he can be very funny. There's also a list of possible names for Alt's famous fried chicken (eventually, he went for Aldo). During lunch or dinner service, he'll move to this or that station, not so much to inspect his brigade's work, but rather to play with some new technique.

Today he's tweaking his base concept, something he's been developing for years. A base is a soft, versatile paste or cream obtained by processing one specific ingredient (he has used pistachio, almond, tomato, even shrimp heads) into its purest form. Today he's trying a brand of superlative artisanal pasta: he cooks it in water, with some white wine vinegar, then purées it. The result is a pure pasta "canvas," a perfect vessel for flavor. He finishes it with *peperone crusco* (a fried dried sweet pepper), capers, sundried tomatoes, garlic, chili powder, vinegar and preserved lemon, then spoons it over some trenette pasta (again, the layering). I take a forkful: it's the color of cooked lobster, creamy, luscious. It's pasta at the one hundredth degree, one of the best dishes I've ever had. "You taste everything, there is no interference," he smiles. "There's no condiments, either: think about the possibilities!"

Cristiana is often the first to taste her brother's new dishes. She knows the way Niko's mind and palate work like no one else. On the rare occasion something is off in a dish she catches it the moment it lands at the pass. No imperfect plate of food has ever found its way onto one of Cristiana Romito's exquisite silver trays, let alone to her dining room. She's a very private person, with a quirky, pungent sense of humor, elegant and feisty: there's a reason why her husband Fabio nicknamed her "peperoncino reale."

Gaia Giordano is another key player on Romito's team. Born in Rome, she discovered her love of cooking while studying to become a judge. She trained as a sommelier, then enrolled in culinary school. After working at Il Convivio Troiani, in Rome, she met Romito; she's been his right arm since 2012, overseeing all of the projects falling under the umbrella of Spazio, which means also supervising the graduates of Accademia Niko Romito; they all spend periods of time in her kitchens as part of their internships.

Educating the next generations of Italian chefs is one of Romito's main objectives. He has found a new space, a forty-three-thousand square foot former furniture outlet between Casadonna and Alt: he plans to move the Accademia there. While showing me around he explains there will be four main areas of study: nutritional science, restaurant format development, catering. And cucina italiana. "There's so much to teach, still, when it comes to that. We have to re-code everything, systemically. Flavor is everything; it has to be precise, neat, vertical, and we can't separate it from nutrition. To do all this, we must master technique. Tradition will be a source of inspiration, for the food and the experience of food, but we need to be contemporary as well. Trattoria is the starting point. I can't tell you what the end point will be yet."

We finish our chat at Alt, mingling with the usual crowd, families, truck drivers, local personalities. They've come for the *pollo fritto* (which is cooked in a pressurized fryer that looks like it belongs at NASA), for Bomba, for the vegetables and ribs barbecued on a Josper grill, for the pizza bianca with local charcuterie and cheese. Little by little, they all come say hi to Niko. "You're like Mother Teresa," I joke. I ask him if people ever ask him to bless their kids. "I don't know if they think I'm blessing them, but they do ask me to hold them, and then take pictures," he replies, with one of his silvery laughs.

In a few years, it will be clear that there's a "Before and After Niko Romito" in Italian cooking. Maybe more than a Mother Teresa, he's a culinary Jesus.

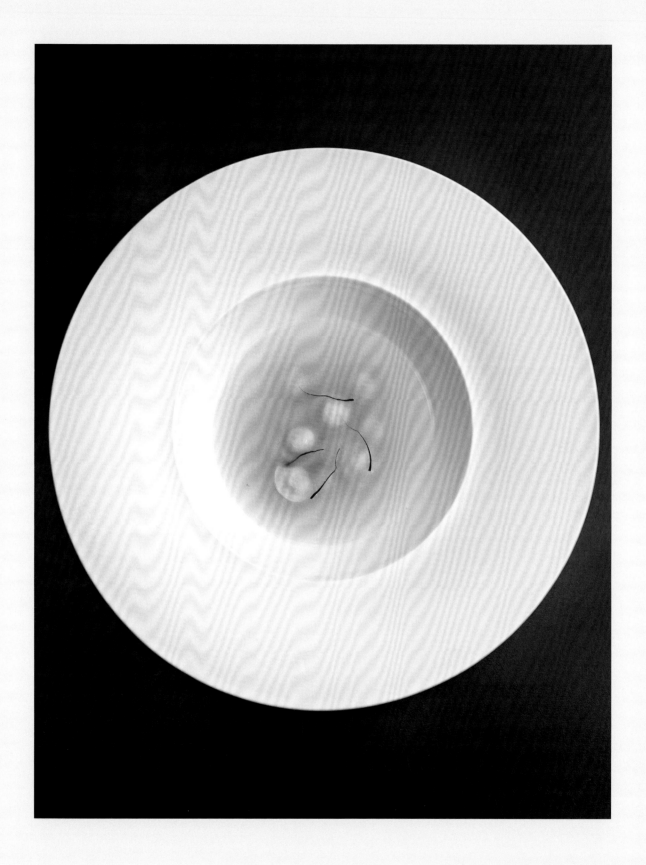

Assoluto di Cipolle, Parmigiano e Zafferano Tostato

"Absolute" Onion with Parmesan-filled Pasta Buttons and Toasted Saffron

Ten years ago, Assoluto di Cipolle marked a new phase for pasta ripiena in brodo (fresh filled pasta served in a broth) in the Italian culinary landscape. Both the dish and the use of the word "assoluto," which indicates the purest form of a specific ingredient, have been widely imitated in the past few years. Instead of broth, Romito uses an onion extraction, which is 100% onion, in a liquid form with no water added (he obtains this with a professional extractor, but you can replicate it at home with a food processor and a fine mesh sieve). Saffron, which Romito gets from a small producer located on the Piana di Navelli, is a prized specialty of Abruzzo, and is picked by hand. Romito toasts the pistils to reduce the transfer of flavor to the broth, while intensifying the aromatic notes. Each spoonful is different, depending on whether you pick up one, two, or all three of the distinctive elements in your bite.

1 cup (3.5 oz.) freshly grated Parmigiano Reggiano
3 tablespoons heavy cream
Fresh egg pasta sheets (recipe follows)
2 cups rock salt or coarse kosher salt
4.5 lbs. medium yellow onions
¼ teaspoon pure vitamin C powder (ascorbic acid)
Salt
½ teaspoon white wine vinegar, or to taste
12 saffron pistils

Special equipment:
¾ inch ring mold or round cookie cutter
Cheesecloth

Serves 4

Stir together the Parmigiano Reggiano and heavy cream until a smooth, dense paste forms. With your hands, form tiny balls from the cheese mixture, about the size of a small chickpea. Lay a sheet of fresh pasta dough on a clean work surface and cut in half lengthwise. Starting from the short edge, place balls of the Parmigiano mixture down the length, spacing them an inch apart. Brush dough around the filling lightly with water and gently press down on the filling with your thumb to flatten the Parmigiano balls into button shapes. Top with second half of dough, pressing around each mound with your fingertips to seal and push out any air pockets. Using a ¾-inch ring mold or round cookie cutter, cut around the buttons, only slightly wider than the filling. Press around the edges with fingertips to seal again if necessary. Repeat with remaining dough and filling. Gently transfer finished buttons to a tray lightly dusted with semolina and refrigerate, uncovered, overnight.

Preheat oven to 325°F. Line an 11x13 inch baking dish with parchment paper and cover the bottom with an even layer of rock salt or coarse kosher salt. Arrange the unpeeled onions on top of the salt; cover the dish tightly with aluminum foil and place in preheated oven. Cook without disturbing for 1 hour and 30 minutes.

Remove from oven, discard aluminum foil, and let cool to room temperature. When onions are cool enough to handle, peel then place them in a food processor and blend until smooth. Pour the blended onions into a fine mesh sieve set over a wide bowl and let drain for at least 1 hour, stirring occasionally. Transfer the strained pulp to a large piece of cheesecloth, gather up the corners to create a pouch, and squeeze forcefully over the bowl to release all the liquid from the pulp. Add salt and vinegar to the onion extraction, taste and adjust flavors accordingly.

Preheat oven to 150°F, or lowest heat setting. Place the saffron on a parchment-lined baking tray and dry in preheated oven for 2 to 5 minutes.

Heat onion extraction in a small saucepan over medium heat until steaming, but do not boil. Bring a large pot of water to a boil over high heat; add 3 tablespoons salt. Cook ravioli for 1 to 2 minutes, or until they float to the surface. Drain in a colander. Divide ravioli between warm, shallow bowls and cover with a ladleful of onion extraction. Gently place 3 toasted saffron threads on the surface of the broth; serve immediately.

Fresh Egg Pasta
3 ½ cups (17 oz.) 00 flour
4 large eggs
5 large egg yolks
½ teaspoon white wine vinegar

Special equipment:
Pasta machine

Makes 4 pasta sheets

Pour the flour into a large bowl, create a mound with a crater in the center. Add the eggs, egg yolks, and vinegar to the crater; use your fingers or a fork to gradually mix the eggs into the flour until it comes together in a crumbly mass. Pour onto a lightly floured work surface and knead for 5 to 7 minutes until the dough is very smooth and elastic. If it is sticky, knead in a teaspoon of flour at a time until it doesn't stick to your hands when touched. Wrap tightly in plastic wrap and allow it to relax in the refrigerator for 30 minutes to 1 hour.

Remove dough from refrigerator and discard plastic wrap. Cut the dough into 4 pieces and flatten each piece into a rough rectangle. Lightly dust the rollers of a pasta machine with flour and pass one piece of dough through the machine on the largest setting (keep other pieces of dough covered with plastic wrap in the meantime, to avoid drying them out). Fold the dough in thirds and pass through the rollers again. Continue rolling the dough through the machine, dusting with flour as necessary and adjusting to a smaller setting each time, until the sheet is very thin, about 1 mm. Transfer pasta sheet to a flour-dusted work surface and cover with a clean kitchen towel. Repeat with remaining dough.

Cavolfiore Gratinato
Roasted Cauliflower

This cauliflower marks the continuation of Romito's work on vegetable-only main courses and also on the layering of different versions of the same ingredient (in this case it's marinated cauliflower, glazed with cauliflower, on top of a cauliflower purée base). The Cavolfiore Gratinato followed his famous Verza e Patate (Roasted Savoy Cabbage and Potatoes), where, similarly, the cabbage was marinated and matured. This procedure benefits both the flavor and texture of the vegetable, as fermentation begins to occur and the interior becomes increasingly meaty and compact, while developing a certain creaminess.

4 ½ cauliflower heads (about 2 lbs. per full head), divided
Salt
1/3 cup sugar, divided
2 2/3 cup extra virgin olive oil, divided, plus more for serving
2 cups dry white wine, divided
Scant 1 cup white wine vinegar, plus more to taste
1 tablespoon butter
½ teaspoon Dijon mustard, or to taste

Special Equipment:
Half-gallon size zipper-topped plastic bags
Cheesecloth

Serves 4

For the marinated cauliflower
Preheat oven to 225°F. Wash and pat dry 4 cauliflower heads and cut them in half through the central stalk. Wrap each half in a piece of parchment paper and then a piece of aluminum foil, gathering at the top but leaving partially open. To each of the 8 packets add: 1 teaspoon salt, 2 teaspoons sugar, 1/3 cup olive oil, ¼ cup white wine, and 1 tablespoon plus 2 teaspoons white wine vinegar. Close packets tightly and transfer to two baking sheets. Cook in preheated oven until just tender but not falling apart, about 1 hour. Fill a large tub (or several large bowls) with ice water. When the cauliflower have finished baking, immediately transfer each packet to a zipper-topped plastic bag, seal tightly and place in ice bath until completely cool. Remove bags from ice bath and transfer to the refrigerator for 3 days.

For the cauliflower glaze
After 3 days, open bags and unwrap cauliflower halves. Set aside 2 for serving, and reserve ½ cup of liquid from the packets. Working in batches, transfer the remaining 6 to a blender or mixer, along with 6 cups of water. Blend until smooth. Filter the mixture using cheesecloth; gather up the corners and squeeze to release liquid into a wide bowl. Discard solids. Transfer filtered cauliflower liquid to a medium saucepan and cook over high heat, stirring often, until sauce has thickened considerably and is a light caramel color; 35 to 45 minutes.

For the cauliflower base
Dice the remaining raw half cauliflower. Melt the butter in a medium-large frying pan over high heat. Add cauliflower and cook, stirring occasionally, until golden and tender, 7 to 10 minutes. Remove from heat, transfer to a blender and blend until smooth. Add up to a tablespoon of water if needed, to reach a thick, spoonable purée. Add mustard, salt, and vinegar to taste; blend again until well combined.

To finish
Preheat oven to 500°F. Cut the 2 reserved, marinated cauliflower halves in half again; you will have 4 cauliflower wedges. Place the wedges on a parchment-lined baking sheet and brush with the reserved cooking liquid. Roast in preheated oven for 5 minutes, or until golden and hot. Remove from oven; brush with the reduced cauliflower glaze, and drizzle with olive oil.

Dollop a spoonful of cauliflower base in the center of each of four plates, top with a glazed cauliflower wedge, and serve immediately.

Pane con Patate di Niko Romito
Niko Romito's Sourdough-Potato Bread

Romito has done extensive work on bread: not only is a division of his company devoted to continuous research on wheat varieties (he produces a bread with two local heritage varieties of wheat, Solina and Saragolla) and the science of dough, with a 1,000-loaf-per-day production rate, but he was also the first chef in Italy to serve bread as its own course at his three Michelin star restaurant, Reale. What follows in the adaptation of the first bread recipe he developed: it incorporates potatoes, which are used in many farming households (potatoes lock in extra humidity, keeping the crumb moist for longer) in the center and south of Italy. The original recipe calls for type 0 flour: in order to come as close to that as possible we used a blend of unbleached all-purpose and stoneground white whole-wheat all-purpose flour. In addition, the recipe called for some semola rimacinata: while some U.S. stores will carry that, you can replace it with durum semolina. Be aware that the addition of potato makes for a dough that is stickier than usual.

1 medium Russet or baking potato (5 oz.), scrubbed
3½ cups (14 oz.) stoneground whole wheat all-purpose flour
3 1/3 cups (14 oz.) unbleached all-purpose flour
1¼ cups (7 oz.) fine durum wheat semolina
1 cup active sourdough levain (recipe follows), roughly 3 to 4 hours after last feeding
3 1/3 cups lukewarm water
2 tablespoons salt

Special equipment:
Dutch oven
Lame or razor blade (or very sharp, small knife)
Bench knife

Makes 2 loaves

Pour about one inch of water into a pot with a fitted steamer basket. Place over medium heat and add potato to steamer basket. Cover pot tightly and steam until potato is very tender, 30 to 40 minutes. Peel and mash the potato with a potato ricer or masher. Set aside to cool completely, about 45 minutes.

Stir together flours and semolina, add mashed potato and mix well. Stir in levain and 2½ cups of water; begin mixing by hand until water is absorbed and a shaggy mass has formed. Cover with a clean dishcloth and let rest for 20 minutes. (This process is called autolyse and helps develop the gluten matrix.)

Sprinkle salt over the surface of dough. Wet hands with some of the remaining water and sprinkle over the salt, rubbing with your hands until salt dissolves. Pull a portion of the dough from the edge of the bowl and fold into the center of the dough, rotate bowl and continue pulling from the edge and tucking into the center until salt is well incorporated (this is called the "stretch and fold" method). Begin adding remaining water one tablespoon at a time, pulling the edges of the dough and folding into the center. Work dough until water is completely incorporated before adding another tablespoon of water. If dough begins to feel saturated before adding all the water, wet your hands with some of the remaining water, sprinkle and rub over the surface of dough, pressing lightly with fingers and let rest for 3 minutes before continuing to work it into the dough. You may have ¼ cup of water leftover when the dough stops accepting water.

Cover with a clean cloth and set aside for bulk fermentation—the dough should almost double in size and show surface bubbles; this will take between 4 to 5 hours, depending on the room temperature. During this stage, fold the dough once every 45 minutes using the "coil fold" method: Slide wet hands under the dough and gently pick it up from the center so the two ends tuck under the center of the dough. Remove hands, rotate bowl 90° and repeat process. Stop folding after 3 or 4 hours, depending on how long the bulk fermentation takes.

Pre-shape the dough: Dump onto a clean, dry surface, preferably wooden or steel. Lightly dust the dough with flour (do not flour the work surface). Using a bench knife, divide the dough in half. Push one portion of the dough towards your lightly floured hand with the bench knife, using your bare hand to guide and tuck the dough under itself as you push, working the dough into a taut round. The motion should be quick and gentle. Set aside pre-shaped loaf, and repeat with the other portion of dough. Let loaves rest for 20 minutes. (This is called "bench rest" and it helps the dough relax before shaping.)

Shape the loaves: Dust two 9-inch bread-proofing baskets with semolina flour (alternatively, line a bowl with a clean dish cloth and dust with semolina flour). Use a bench knife to flip one loaf over onto a clean, lightly-floured work surface. Starting at the side closest to you, pull and stretch the bottom 2 corners of the dough down toward you, then fold them up into the middle of the dough. Repeat on both sides, pulling the edges out and folding them into the center. Finally, lift the top edge up and fold down over previous folds. Flip dough over so the folded side is underneath and shape into a smooth, taut round with your hands. Transfer loaf, flipping so it is seam-side up, to prepared basket or bowl. Repeat the entire procedure with the other loaf. Transfer both loaves to refrigerator to proof overnight.

The next morning, place a covered cast-iron Dutch oven inside oven, and preheat to 475°F . Cut a round of parchment paper roughly the size of the bottom of the Dutch oven. When oven is hot, take one loaf from refrigerator. Flip the loaf over onto the parchment paper round and score the surface of the loaf lengthwise in one swift, firm movement with your lame or sharp knife. Grabbing the sides of the parchment, carefully transfer the loaf to the Dutch oven (the sides of the Dutch oven will be very hot!). Cover and bake in hot oven, for 25 minutes.

Uncover the Dutch oven, and lower oven temperature to 425°F. Finish baking, uncovered, until the crust is golden-brown and the bottom of the loaf sounds hollow if you knock on it, 20 to 25 minutes more. Carefully remove loaf from Dutch oven, transfer to a cooling rack for at least 20 minutes before cutting into it. Repeat process with remaining loaf.

Sourdough Starter
Note on terminology: I am following Tartine's Chad Robertson's choice of calling "starter" the pre-fermented flour and water mix which is fed daily and "levain" as the portion of starter that will go into the final dough.

½ cup white whole wheat all-purpose flour
½ cup water, room temperature

Special equipment:
Mason jar with lid, clean and dry, or small food safe plastic container, with lid

Combine flour and water in the mason jar until texture is creamy (depending on the type of flour, you might find yourself with some leftover water). Leave the jar open for 20 minutes. Close the jar and leave to rest in a warm place for 48 hours, after which you should check for signs of activated fermentation: small surface bubbles and a smell with fresh and mildly acidic notes, like yogurt, and/or sweeter ones, like a ripe banana. Once these are observed, you have obtained your starter, which you can now begin feeding: Discard about 1/3 of the starter, add 1/3 cup fresh flour and 1/3 cup water (at room temperature) until texture is creamy. Close the lid and repeat every day (this should be done roughly at the same time each day, at least for the first month). After each feeding, you should observe a rise in the starter's level—it's a sign of correct fermentation. Make sure you leave enough room in the jar after each feeding for expansion of the starter.

It's advisable to wait at least three to four weeks before attempting to make bread with a new starter. When you're ready to try, double your daily feedings (morning and evening) for 2 to 3 days prior to making bread. On the day you're making bread, prepare your levain by feeding your starter (make sure the final amount is more than 1 cup, so you have enough to use for your recipe, and some left to rebuild your starter) and waiting roughly 4 hours; when the levain's rising is at its peak, you can proceed.

We recommend building your own starter culture when the weather is warm, as environmental temperature influences fermentation.

Melanzana e Pomodoro in Agrodolce
Sweet and Sour Eggplant and Tomato

This recipe is an homage to one of the signature dishes of Niko Romito's restaurant Reale (roasted eggplant, tomato, and peach caramel), and is an example of how that three-Michelin-starred restaurant and the more casual Spazio share a common culinary philosophy. As in the original dish, bitter, sweet, acidic, and balsamic notes play together harmoniously and the eggplant's texture is almost meaty.

Onion
½ cup white wine vinegar
¼ teaspoon sugar
1 red onion, cut in half lengthwise

Eggplant
1 medium eggplant, about ¾ lb.
Salt

Tomatoes
Two 14.5 oz. cans of whole peeled tomatoes
¼ teaspoon salt
¼ teaspoon sugar
¼ teaspoon lemon zest
½ teaspoon fresh thyme, chopped
1 tablespoon extra-virgin olive oil
1 tablespoon plus 1 teaspoon white wine vinegar
2 tablespoons honey

To finish
8 green olives, pitted and quartered
2 tablespoons small, salt-packed capers, soaked in water and rinsed
Cayenne pepper
3 sprigs of thyme
3 sprigs of marjoram
1 sprig of rosemary
1 tablespoon extra-virgin olive oil
Salt, to taste
Fresh basil leaves

Serves 2

For the onion
Stir together vinegar and sugar in a small bowl. Use a paring knife to peel off the outer two layers of each onion half, and set aside the rest of the onion for another use. Submerge the two onion pieces in the vinegar mixture and set aside to marinate at room temperature for 1 hour. Drain and pat dry with paper towels. Thinly slice the onion pieces lengthwise; set aside.

For the eggplant
Bring a large pot of water to a boil over high heat, and add a tablespoon of salt. Trim the eggplant and slice in half lengthwise. Cook eggplant in boiling water until you can easily insert a sharp knife into the pulp, 7 to 10 minutes; drain and set aside to cool.

For the tomatoes
Strain the tomatoes in a colander set over a bowl; save the liquid. Place the drained tomatoes in a small bowl; season with salt, sugar, lemon zest, and fresh thyme.

Heat a medium-large nonstick frying pan or skillet over high heat. Add the tomatoes to the hot, dry pan and cook, stirring occasionally until browned on all sides, about 5 to 7 minutes. Purée tomatoes in a mixer or blender with 1 tablespoon olive oil, then press through a fine mesh strainer, collecting sauce in a small bowl. Transfer the pulp to a piece of cheesecloth and squeeze to release all of the liquid into the bowl. Discard pulp. You should have about ½ cup of sauce. If you have less than this, stir in a bit of the reserved tomato liquid until you have ½ cup. Add vinegar and honey to the sauce, mix well and set aside.

To finish
Combine olives, capers, marinated onion, and cayenne pepper in a small bowl; set aside. Tie together the thyme, marjoram, and rosemary with cooking twine.

Heat a large nonstick frying pan over high heat. Carefully peel the eggplant. Add eggplant halves and herb bundle to the hot, dry pan and cook until the eggplant browns on both sides, about 8 minutes. Remove pan from heat, discard herb bundle. Allow the pan to cool for 2 minutes, then add tomato sauce to the pan with the eggplant. Place pan over medium heat and cook, turning and stirring constantly, until sauce coats and glazes eggplant completely, 7 to 10 minutes. There should be no sauce left in the pan.

Place a basil leaf and half of the olive and onion mixture in the center of each serving plate. Cover with an eggplant half and drizzle with olive oil.

Serve immediately.

Vitello Panato in Carpione
Veal Milanese in "Carpione"

Cotoletta in carpione is a Piedmontese specialty: Gaia Giordano first tried it in a Turin trattoria and loved it so much she thought of adding it to Spazio's menu. She thought the original carpione, made only with wine, vinegar, and herbs, might be too strong for her clients' palates, so she softened it by adding tomato sauce with marinated red onion, plus a generous amount of EVOO for light spiciness and roundness. Plan ahead to allow twelve hours for this dish to chill. The serving temperature is crucial: it has to be cold, so as to better serve the fresh and acidic notes of the dish.

Two 14 oz. cans whole Datterini or cherry tomatoes
1 tablespoon extra-virgin olive oil, plus more for serving
½ red onion, peeled and thinly sliced
10 salt-packed capers, soaked, rinsed, and patted dry
10 black peppercorns
1/3 cup white wine vinegar
8 sage leaves
1 bay leaf
1 teaspoon salt
16 oz. (1 lb.) of veal sirloin, trimmed and cut into 4 slices, or 4 veal cutlets
1 cup dried breadcrumbs
2 eggs
Salt
Peanut oil, for frying
½ teaspoon cayenne pepper
1 teaspoon caper powder (available online or in specialty stores)

2-4 servings

Purée tomatoes and their juice in a blender or food processor. Strain through a fine mesh sieve, pressing the solids thoroughly with a spatula. Discard solids or set aside for a different use.

Heat 1 tablespoon of olive oil in a medium saucepan over medium heat. Add onion, capers, and peppercorns. Cook, stirring often, until onion begins to soften, about 5 minutes. Add vinegar, strained tomato sauce, sage, and bay leaf. Lower heat to maintain a low simmer and cook, stirring occasionally, for 20 minutes. Remove from heat and set aside to cool.

Meanwhile, pound the meat slices to a uniform thickness with a meat mallet. Break the eggs into a shallow bowl, add a pinch of salt and stir together with a fork. Pour the breadcrumbs onto a separate plate; add a pinch of salt and mix to combine. Dip a slice of meat in the egg mixture, then in the breadcrumbs, pressing to adhere on both sides. Repeat with remaining slices.

Heat a large, nonstick frying pan over medium-high heat. Add about ¼-inch of peanut oil and heat until shimmering. Carefully add the cutlets and cook until golden brown on first side, 1 to 1 ½ minutes, flip, and cook another 1 to 2 minutes. Transfer the cutlets to a paper towel-lined plate, sprinkle lightly with salt, and set aside to cool.

When both the tomato sauce and the cutlets have cooled to room temperature, carefully dip each cutlet in the tomato mixture, turning to coat, and transfer to an airtight container. Cover the cutlets with the remaining tomato sauce, close the container, and refrigerate for 12 hours.

To serve
Remove cutlets from refrigerator 30 minutes before serving. Place one cutlet in the center of a serving plate (be careful to remove any sage or bay leaves), and arrange a few slices of onion and several capers on top. Garnish with cayenne pepper, caper powder, and drizzle with olive oil.

PAOLO

LOPRIORE

Because Paolo Lopriore is a self-proclaimed tech-grouch, he asked if, instead of typing his recipes up and sending them over email, he could simply dictate them to me. So now I'm on the phone with one of Italy's most legendary chefs, trying to get each measurement right but most importantly drinking up his side notes, which I dare say are even more interesting than the recipes themselves.

This is often the case with Lopriore, who is undoubtedly a crucial, if controversial, link between the past and future of Italian gastronomy, having transitioned from Gualtiero Marchesi's rigorous kitchens to the difficult vanguardism of a fine dining chapter at Il Canto, near Siena, and finally to the down-home formats of his last two restaurants (Kitchen and Il Portico), which more than a few talents from the new wave of cucina italiana have visited in search of inspiration. While Lopriore's occasional crypticism and profound shyness make him ineligible to play the part of a modern-day Socrates, he certainly has loads of definitive concepts to pass on regarding flavor, service, and identity. Many young guns use "Lopriorisms" without even being aware of their origin: the true sign he has left his mark.

But let's take this back a few months. As I walk into the open plan kitchen of Il Portico, in Appiano Gentile, near Como, I'm greeted by Rosa. "Mia mamma!" says Lopriore, who's right behind her. Papà Giuseppe works at the restaurant as well. The whole family has finally reunited in the small, sleepy town Giuseppe and Rosa have called home for many decades (she's originally from Naples, he's from Bari). Their prodigal son has returned to find peace.

45

The New Cucina Italiana

He wasn't always peaceful. When the teenage Lopriore started his first kitchen stint with "il signor Marchesi" (as he calls him), at the maestro's historic restaurant on Via Bonvesin della Riva in Milan, he didn't even know who Gualtiero Marchesi was. But he soaked his lessons up, before moving to another fine dining temple, Enoteca Pinchiorri, in Florence. He rejoined his mentor for the project of a Franciacorta restaurant, at L'Albereta, once again after a few years. In the middle there were experiences at Pavillon Ledoyen and Maison Troigros, in France, and in Norway.

Then came his solo debut. At Il Canto, in a former monastery outside of Siena, he served daring, angular food some people found offensive, others inspirational. Dishes that were at once ascetic and sumptuous, like a seaweed, herb, and root salad, to be eaten with one's hands; a tomato paste brick served with licorice and bottarga (cured fish roe); duck breast with pine nut sauce, anchovies, gentian and pine honey. He earned, then lost, a Michelin star, was promoted, then demoted, by a few gastronomic guides; though many of his colleagues praised his work, he wasn't popular: perhaps he was too far ahead of the curve. After a couple of short-lived openings (one in Milan, one on Lake Como), it was time for Il Portico.

"French cuisine taught us to build vegetables into courses, as if they were an integral part of the dish, and we're having trouble separating them again." Lopriore is talking about the necessity to reclaim contorni (sides) as proper courses, while frying a heap of zucchini; he will finish them with a Scapece sauce, a traditional vinegar and wine-based marinade, and raisins (recipe on page 53). He speaks of zucchini with great fondness. As someone who doesn't drive, he often takes the train and loves seeing them grown in communal gardens by the tracks. "Restoring autonomy to vegetables is something more pertinent to the spirit of the Italian center or south, not so much up here. But I like when you can pick vegetables up by the forkful. On my convivial table, they are presented as a course, cooked al dente, but also fried and braised. People can serve themselves from the communal dish."

This convivial table is the key to Lopriore's most recent culinary chapter, something he's been building towards for the past few years. While still at Il Canto, he had started dialing down the extremisms in his dishes, exposing the familiar elements that had always been at their core (for those who caught them). Then he started collaborating with the late Lucchese artist Andrea Salvetti on a series of sculptural serving devices that allowed food to be partially cooked at the table, and taken by customers in the amount they desired.

Long before this became known (and cool) as "shared plates" style, it was "family style," the way food was served at home. It still is, in many homes. And yet it's a format foreigners seem to be able to connect to more easily than Italians: for us, says Lopriore, how quickly one gets food at the restaurant (and how much food one gets) is more important than the details of how the food is served. The latter is precisely what interests him. "At Portico we don't use many of Salvetti's pieces anymore, because we feel the ornamental element had become overpowering, but we still serve each element separately: pasta, rice, meat, fish, sides, condiments; people assemble their own dishes, and maybe the way you make yours is better than mine, and I will have a second serving, building my plate the way you did. This style of service fosters an exchange among tablemates." So, actually, this is not "sharing": dishes are not finished and then served in one plate for the whole table to partake; dishes are assembled at the table, on each guest's plate, as he or she chooses among a variety of building blocks.

The question is: if a chef's work stops before plating (which is not just a matter of aesthetics, but also of proportion: how much of this, how much of that) how exactly can his work be judged? "Eh, yes, judging

becomes difficult. With Salvetti I learned my role, as a chef, is to master the art of cooking. I have to be quick to 'freeze' that instant, when the food is ready, and send it off. Stop."

We move to the garden, to a beautiful Danish-built customized brazier with a pile of fresh wood and an adjustable metallic arm where meat is hung to cook, first closer to the fire, then raised, like an asado crucificado (an Argentinian technique involving strapping whole carcasses to metal crosses and grilling them). Once the fire has died down, Lopriore slow-cooks some tajine for the Sunday lunch. The menu changes every day; lunch costs 18 Euros.

"Once a client brought me a couple of geese and asked if I could roast them for him. It wasn't easy, but I would like to do it again." I love the idea of Lopriore roasting goose, because no one does it anymore, and it's so Italian. I also love that his clients feel comfortable bringing him special ingredients to cook (they often leave fresh bunches of herbs outside the door, too), now and then, as if he were an innkeeper. "It's the reason why I keep old cookbooks in the kitchen: if someone requests some long-forgotten preparation, I have to look it up." ("What about Google?" "Oh, I don't use that.")

Lopriore barbecues on Saturdays, because that's when his clientele, which is mostly local, likes to eat barbecue. It's the lesson he learned from Troigros and Marchesi: cook for your regulars (or your territory) first, then for whomever else will come. He calls it *cucina di microclima*, where "microclimate" refers to local food habits, to knowing which flavors his people crave. It doesn't automatically mean a "zero food mile" approach: Lopriore gets his vegetables from a nearby convent, where missionary nuns employ growing techniques they learned in Africa, and his fish from Lake Como, but he also uses supermarket pasta and an everyday brand of coffee. "I'm a maniac when it comes to fresh ingredients, and we do make a lot of fresh pasta in-house, but with prepackaged foods I have a pretty loose approach. I do believe Italy has the best food processing industry: it's because it follows our palate, which is a natural quality detector."

Lopriore uses a mortar to puree his herbs, grates garlic on a piece of shark skin a young Japanese chef gave him (he adds a couple of dollops of pulp with a toothpick to his tomato sauce: he says it's more digestible this way). His version of technology is deciding which pan to use: iron, steel, or copper. Technique he knows well, technology he doesn't like: it only makes sense when working with big numbers. Il Portico is not El Bulli. Chamber quartet versus symphonic orchestra. Lopriore's idea of a perfectly Italian restaurant dessert is *una coppa di gelato con frutta*. "You know, in the end Adrià was a genius because no matter how futuristic his cuisine was, the format was still tapas, something the Spanish could identify immediately."

A group of friends have come to have aperitivo at the counter (it's not noon yet). Lopriore greets them, then shows his small brigade how to make puff pastry while he talks about Italian sauces. "They're the backbone of our cuisine. Through the magical element of time we concentrate flavors. Use the lid: let your food dry, then hydrate it, then let it dry again. Never let the casserole dominate you: you're in charge, as you lower or raise the flame. This is how we create umami." In the basement, he keeps a paper target, a hand-drawn triangle connecting three C's, which stand for cucina, cameriere, cliente (kitchen, waiter, guest). Every day he throws darts at it and depending on where they land, he gauges which to pay more or less attention to.

Lopriore teaches at Alma, Italy's most respected institute for higher culinary education. He also teaches by example, whenever a group of young chefs visit him: they sit and watch him as he cooks. "We talk about flavor a lot. Tradition is inevitably a chef's starting point when building new dishes, but the real lesson we absorb from home cooking is flavor matching, more than recipes. From my grandmother, for instance, I learned to add walnuts to a fish sauce: it's what she'd make every year on Christmas Eve." Like an instinctive taste-compatibility app: all the matriarchs and patriarchs of cooking, all over the world, have it. In our country, it speaks our language. Chefs, as professionals, build on that knowledge—but with better techniques.

Mastering the art of Italian flavor means making dishes that are recognizable, no matter what form they take. You can turn a lasagna inside out, but people should be able eat it and immediately think "it's lasagna" without having to look for it on the plate. Lopriore thinks this is something our new generation of chefs (or at least the ones he likes) seems to understand. He appreciates their ingenuity: they're opening restaurants without big investors backing them, with their own money, because they've chosen it as a career and they believe in it. It's not a marketing operation. "But they need to stay in their kitchens: from what I see they move around too much, attend too many events; then they become complacent and unfocused, and their creativity suffers."

Paolo Lopriore could have been one of Italy's most acclaimed culinary stars, with tv shows, commercials, chains of restaurants, book deals, and a sophisticated clientele. His brush with the gastronomic arena has left him scarred (you can see it in the occasional twitching of his arm). He has chosen to go back home because that's where he feels safe at this particular moment of his life, where he can make the kind of food he likes. As the town's church bells ring the hour, I ask him if he's happy. He smiles: "I am."

Riso in Cagnone, Pesce di Lago e Condimenti
Rice "in Cagnone," Lakefish, and Condiments

Lopriore's philosophy is perfectly represented by this recipe, in which a local fish is served with rice and condiments, the individual elements assembled by each guest to her or his liking directly at the table. The rice preparation—not a risotto, as risotto is not common in Lopriore's native area—is similar to a pilaf. In cagnone is a method of cooking typical of Lombardy and Piedmont, in which rice is boiled and then sautéed in butter until brown. Lopriore was inspired by the movie *Jiro Dreams of Sushi* to make his rice in a pressure cooker which breaks down the grains and completely releases their starch; the resulting texture is similar to that of sushi rice. Lopriore likes to coat his with almond "crumbs" leftover from the extraction of sweet and bitter almonds.

2 ½ cups Carnaroli rice
1 stick plus 6 tablespoons unsalted butter, cut into pieces
1 teaspoon salt, plus more to taste
Lakefish (recipe follows)
Bay Leaf Concentrate (recipe follows)
Clove-Scented Hollandaise (recipe follows)
Zucchine in Scapece (see next page)

Special equipment:
Pressure cooker

Serves 4

Rinse rice under cold water until the water runs clear. Place rice in a pressure cooker and cover with 1 inch of cold water. Scatter the butter pieces over the surface of the water, lock the lid, and place over high heat. Cook at high pressure for 7 minutes, remove from heat and do a quick-release of the pressure. Open lid and fluff rice with a fork. Serve right away with Lakefish, Bay Leaf Concentrate, and Clove-Scented Hollandaise.

Lakefish
If the fish is extremely fresh (as in, has been pulled out of the lake just minutes or a few hours before preparing), Lopriore suggests steaming the filets. Otherwise, the following preparation is recommended.

5 tablespoons butter
8 fillets of tench, carp, or other freshwater fish
Salt

Melt 2 tablespoons of butter in a large nonstick frying pan over medium-high heat. Add 4 fish fillets, sprinkle with salt and cook, flipping once, until the surface of each fillet is white and the interior is still slightly translucent (time will vary according to size and type of fish used). Transfer cooked fish to a plate and repeat with another 2 tablespoons of butter and remaining 4 fillets. Transfer to the plate and add the remaining tablespoon of butter to the pan, stirring to melt into the fish juices. Drizzle buttery pan juices over fish and serve immediately.

Bay Leaf Concentrate
8 fresh bay leaves, rinsed
½ cup water

Combine the bay leaves and water in a blender or food processor and blend on high speed until bay leaves are pulverized. Filter through a fine mesh sieve set over a glass jar. Cover the jar and set aside in a dark place for several hours or overnight, until a green concentrate forms on the bottom and separates from the water on top. Pour off the water and save the concentrate.

Clove-Scented Hollandaise
10 cloves
½ teaspoon plus 2 tablespoons water, divided
3 egg yolks
Salt
1 stick of butter plus 2 tablespoons, at room temperature and cut into 8 pieces
1 ½ teaspoon white wine vinegar
Crush the cloves into a fine powder using a mortar and pestle or spice grinder. Transfer to a small bowl and combine with ½ teaspoon water; stir to form a smooth paste. Add more water if necessary to reach desired consistency. Filter through a fine mesh sieve; set aside.

Combine egg yolks, a pinch of salt, and 2 tablespoons of water in a heatproof bowl set over a pan of barely simmering water. Whisk mixture vigorously until it thickens slightly. Remove from heat and add butter one piece at a time, stirring constantly until melted. Heat bowl again over simmering water, and stir until it thickens and turns bright yellow, 5 to 7 minutes. Gradually whisk in the vinegar and clove paste. Taste for salt and adjust seasoning. Serve warm.

Zucchine in Scapece
Fried Zucchini in "Scapece"

Paolo Lopriore suggests trying different kinds of vinegar for his scapece marinade, such as red wine or raspberry, and recommends using garlic of the highest quality, like the prized garlic from Sulmona in Abruzzo. (Lopriore gets his from his aunt Maddalena, who produces it exclusively for the family.) Adding fresh herbs to the zucchini while still warm draws out the aromatic notes.

8 zucchini
4 cups rock salt or coarse kosher salt
2 cups water
2 cups white wine vinegar
1/3 cup dry white wine
¼ cup sugar
5 cups canola oil, for frying
10 mint leaves
10 basil leaves
2 garlic cloves, peeled and halved

Serves 4, or 6 to 8 as a side dish

Trim off ends and cut each zucchini crosswise into 3-inch chunks. Arrange the zucchini in a single layer in a plastic container and cover completely with the rock salt. Let stand at room temperature for 2 hours.

Meanwhile, combine water, vinegar, wine, and sugar in a medium saucepan over medium heat. Cook, stirring frequently, until sugar is dissolved, 5 to 10 minutes. Remove from heat, pour into a bowl, and set aside to cool.

After 2 hours, remove zucchini from salt, brush off excess with a pastry brush or paper towels (do not rinse zucchini with water at this point). Heat the oil in a large, deep pot or wok over high heat. The oil is ready when a cube of bread sizzles immediately when dropped in. Fry the zucchini in the hot oil for 8 to 10 minutes over high heat, then reduce heat to low and cook 3 to 5 minutes, until the skin is wrinkled and crisp and the zucchini are cooked through. Transfer with a spider or slotted spoon to a paper towel-lined plate to let cool.

Add zucchini to bowl with the cooled marinade. Toss in the mint, basil, and garlic; set aside for 1 hour. Drain zucchini before serving.

JURI CRIOTTI
ALICE DELCOURT
LUCA GRASSELLI
DAMIANO DONATI
ALESSANDRO MIOCCHI
GIUSEPPE LO LUDICE
FRATELLI MONTARULI

FARMERS & FORAGERS

JURI

CHIOTTI

The gelato is bananas. Perched precariously on top of a thick waffle cone are two humongous scoops, two flavors: hay (hand-cut hay, with its intoxicating aroma of wildflowers) and local blueberry. It's the creamiest gelato I've ever had, with the purest taste, like fresh mountain milk drunk from a wooden bucket: clean, grassy, nutty, and fatty. It's substantial, nutritious, not too rich: the moment you've finished it you could eat more. Which I do. Chamomile and hazelnut.

This is Fioca ("snow" in local dialect), an artisanal gelateria opened in a small Piedmontese town not far from France by a team of smart kids: the partners behind Officina Antagonisti (a local "beer firm") and Juri Chiotti, a young chef from these valleys who left, earned a Michelin star, and returned to rebuild the local economy with the help of a community of like-minded artisans. His restaurant, Reis Cibo Libero di Montagna ("reis" here means "roots"), is in a two-story cabin up a winding mountain road, surrounded by woods, with a striking view of the valley below. The closest village is Frassino, named after the indigenous ash trees, whose leaves have been used for centuries to supply fat and protein to cattle feed.

The next day, we travel to Cresco, a permaculture project that produces more than a hundred varieties of seedlings, including many heirloom ones, that Lorenzo "Fiore" Barra started after taking a year off from accounting to travel the world. Juri maintains his own vegetable garden and between what he grows, what Lorenzo delivers, and what he gets from his dad, also a horticulturist, he's completely self-sufficient. Self-sufficiency is the key to the bigger project he's been working on for the past few years: creating a mountain community where people produce everything they need to live and thrive; brewers, winemakers, cooks, cheesemongers, herders, farmers, millers, bakers, carpenters, blacksmiths at work, with minimum impact on the local ecosystem. The people from Officina Antagonisti, Lorenzo, Gian Vittorio Porasso of La Servaja, who makes cheese with raw milk from his herd of goats, near the border with of Liguria, and bakers from nearby Roccasparvera will be the first settlers.

"The point is not romantic idealism," says Juri, who buys electronic locks for his animals' enclosures off Amazon. "The point is to prove that we can reignite local microeconomies in a way that is sustainable both financially and environmentally." Nothing irritates him more than fly-by-the-seat-of-your-pants farming, people doing "the rural thing" because it's trendy. "If the mountain is suddenly 'cool' it's fine by me, just as long as we know mountain life is not fashion, it's hard work." Take his chickens: he has a few specimens of Bionda Piemontese, Livornese, and Bianca di Saluzzo, the local breed. They roam free in the underwood, then retreat to their coop to sleep and lay eggs. There are also wolves, but those he rarely sees—a good thing, considering he also has a small herd of sheep. (He summons them from the forest where they graze with an ancestral, hypnotic call.) He has a few Sambucane, a light-boned breed that's kept for meat and wool, with long, meek faces, and the gorgeous Naso Nero del Vallese, with black faces, elbows, knees and hooves, and curly wool. "Between lunch and dinner service, I sit with them: I find it very calming."

The sheep are fed hay and sprouted pea stalks; they also graze on the most tender patches of grass, after goats have already cleared the toughest bushes. Cows finish whatever is left. This way the fields receive three different rounds of manure. Juri's sheep come from a farm in Coumboscuro, another small town about an hour from Frassino. "It's the same farm Diego gets his sheep from," he says. Juri and Diego Rossi, of Trippa (page 198), are friends; they both worked under Norbert Niederkofler at St. Hubertus (now a three-Michelin-star restaurant), in the Dolomites, and eventually became co-executive chefs at Antiche Contrade, in Cuneo. "I like working in tandem, maybe because I am a bit insecure, maybe because I was never interested in being 'the chief.' After some time alone at Antiche Contrade I asked Diego to join for a period, and after two months I asked him to stay for good." Eventually, they were awarded one Michelin star.

Clearly this mountain life suits him better. "One time I set up a tent in front of the humble house of Lucia Rossi, in Borgata San Maurizio, a tiny hamlet abandoned by all except for three elderly couples. I wanted to learn how she makes tumin dal mel, a soft, bloomy, rind cheese made with cow's milk, and in exchange I taught her a recipe for rabbit stew."

Juri calls Lucia his "step-nonna." At seventy-four, there is nothing fragile about her: she was nine years old when she first took the family's cows to pasture. She told me she sometimes thinks of retiring but figures she'd get bored. She still makes the tumin the ancient way. Traditionally, cheesemaking combines two milkings, morning's and night's. But milk would spoil in the heat. So tumin is made twice a day, with fresh milk. Lucia adds whey, and in an hour the cheese is transferred into special molds covered with cotton cloths and stored in a natural cellar for four days: this is how long it takes for the liquids to drain and for the cheese to mature. Juri, who helped establish a Slow Food community in Val Varaita, obtained Presidium status (a Slow Food seal of tutelage) for tumin, which is currently made by just five producers. He also celebrates it at Reis, in a slightly elevated version of raviòlas, a local, oblong version of gnocchi, made with a mix of flour, potatoes, and cheese, and served with a cheese sauce.

Juri makes simple dishes. He has found a balance between playing it safe and going all out and he believes it's what's appropriate for this place. "We have these extraordinary ingredients and we strive to present them

at their best, better than our nonne used to, because we now know more about techniques and products and we would never, say, add too much vinegar to a *finanziera*, a sauce made with offal and scraps, like sweetbreads and cockscombs, or boil tripe for twelve hours, or overcook vegetables. What I have learned from starting in fancy restaurants and working with oysters and foie gras allowed me to do simple, better." His risotto comes with a Barolo reduction and mustardela, a soft local sausage; venison neck is boiled and served with wild spinach and yuzu ponzu; panna cotta is infused with hay and drizzled with pine cone syrup (pages 61 and 63).

Juri is inspired, understandably, by places like Magnus Nilsson's Fäviken, Christian Puglisi's Farm of Ideas, Rodolfo Guzmán's Boragó and Virigilio Martínez's MIL. "I see myself gravitating more and more towards vegetables in the future, though meat will always have a place in my kitchen: whole animals, adult animals, which have already fulfilled their life cycle; I no longer serve baby goat or lamb." His dream is to create a teaching restaurant where people will see how things are grown, bred, handcrafted, before sitting at the table to experience what "his" mountain tastes like.

He points at the slope right in front of Reis, remembering how it used to be covered in rye mixed with wheat, a crossbred crop that was capable of withstanding even the coldest seasons: "If all goes well, we'll sow those seeds again."

Collo di Cervo con Spinaci di Montagna e Ponzu allo Yuzu
Deer Neck with Wild Spinach and Yuzu Ponzu

Deer neck is an often overlooked, potentially tough cut of venison which is transformed in this recipe through a long cooking time in a flavorful broth to yield an exceptionally tender final product. Juri sautés the leaves of the native Good King Henry plant (Chenopodium bonus henricus) as a side dish, but feel free to substitute spinach if you're not in the foraging mood.

Venison
3 carrots, washed and cut into 1-inch chunks
2 yellow onions, peeled and halved
3 celery stalks, washed and cut into 1-inch chunks
3 cloves garlic, peeled
2 fresh or dried bay leaves
1 sprig rosemary, tied with kitchen twine
1 sprig fresh sage
10 dried juniper berries
3 whole cloves
10 black peppercorns
1 tablespoon salt
2.5 lbs. deboned venison neck roast, cut into 4 pieces

To finish
12 cups loosely packed Good King Henry or spinach leaves, washed
Salt
4 tablespoons butter
2 cloves garlic, unpeeled
½ cup yuzu ponzu sauce

Serves 4

For the venison
Combine all ingredients in a large pot, cover generously with cold water and bring to a boil over medium-high heat. Immediately lower heat to maintain a slow simmer for 4 to 5 hours, or until meat is very tender. Remove meat from broth and keep warm. Filter broth with a fine mesh sieve set over a bowl; discard solids.

To finish
Bring a large pot of water to a boil over high heat, add 2 teaspoons of salt. Prepare an ice bath in a large bowl. Boil the spinach leaves for 3 minutes, then transfer to the ice bath with a slotted spoon. Drain in a colander, shaking to rid of excess water. Melt butter in a large frying pan over high heat; when butter is hot add unpeeled garlic and boiled greens. Cook over high heat for 2 to 3 minutes, stirring often; taste for salt and set aside.

Prepare 4 bowls; place a piece of venison in each bowl and pour a ladleful of broth over the meat. Serve hot with sautéed greens on the side, and yuzu ponzu sauce for drizzling.

Panna Cotta al Fieno di Montagna con Sciroppo di Pino Cembro
Hay-Infused Panna Cotta with Pinecone Syrup

Juri Chiotti infuses his panna cotta with mountain hay, but you can substitute an infusion of different herbal teas (we used chamomile, mint, and rose), following the same procedure as the hay infusion, and reducing the steeping time from forty-five to thirty minutes. Plan ahead when making the Pinecone Syrup; the first step is macerating pine cones in sugar for one week in order to draw out their flavor.

2 cups heavy cream
2/3 cup whole milk
1 package (about 1 tablespoon) unflavored, powdered gelatin
¼ cup light honey
¼ cup raw sugar
1 cup dried hay from mountain pastures or herbal tea leaves (see headnote)
Pinecone Syrup (recipe follows)

Serves 6

Combine heavy cream and milk in a small saucepan over medium heat, cook slowly, stirring often, until the mixture is steaming and almost simmering. Remove from heat, add hay (or herbal tea), cover tightly and steep for 45 minutes. Filter the mixture through a fine mesh sieve into a clean saucepan; add sugar and honey and stir to combine.

Pour 2 tablespoons of cold water into a small dish and sprinkle gelatin over the surface of the water. Stir, add 2 tablespoons of the cream mixture; stir again and let stand for 3 to 4 minutes to soften.

Meanwhile set the saucepan with the cream mixture over low heat and cook, stirring often, until mixture is hot and almost simmering; do not let it boil. Remove from heat, whisk in the gelatin mixture until dissolved. Pour the cream mixture into 6 individual ramekins. Cover ramekins with plastic wrap and refrigerate for at least 4 hours, or overnight. Dip bottoms of ramekins in hot water, run a knife around the edges to loosen panna cottas and invert each one onto a small plate. Spoon pinecone syrup over each panna cotta and serve immediately.

Pinecone Syrup
10 small fresh pinecones from a Swiss or stone pine tree
1 ½ cups sugar
½ cup ruby port
1 tablespoon plus 1 teaspoon balsamic vinegar

Cut the pinecones into 4 pieces and place them in a jar. Add the sugar, close the jar and let sit in the sun for about 1 week. Open the jar, add the port, balsamic vinegar, and 2 tablespoons of water; close jar and shake to combine. Filter liquid through a fine mesh sieve into a small saucepan. Bring to a boil over medium-high heat, then reduce to a simmer until reduced to a syrup, about 45 minutes to 1 hour. Set aside to cool at room temperature and then refrigerate until ready to serve.

ALICE

DELCOURT

Chickens, eggs, frogs, cabbages, cheese, and rice: gliding on the Navigli, Milan's famous water canals, slim barges used to carry the country's bounty into the city. This was how the fresh products of Lombardia's *cascine* (farmhouses) and rice fields got to the tables of the industrious middle and upper classes. So much history of my city has run on those canals (they were instrumental in the construction of the Duomo and the printing of *Corriere della Sera*, as marble blocks and paper reels also traveled by boat into the city); only a few have survived, but in their heyday they connected Milan to Lake Maggiore and Lake Como, thanks to a system of sluice gates designed by Leonardo da Vinci. On one of the surviving canals, the Naviglio Pavese (commissioned by Napoleon) sits Erba Brusca, a restaurant that started out with a small vegetable patch in the backyard and now maintains an actual urban microfarm, run by French-American chef Alice Delcourt.

Alice is easy to like: she has the healthy, slightly unkempt beauty I associate with people who are blessed with great genes and also spend a lot of time in nature. I can imagine her surfing, riding horses, maybe even robbing stagecoaches in the Wild West. At the entrance of the restaurant (which she owns with her husband, Danilo Ingannamorte) there's a plaque, inscribed with the motto "Slay" and a sticker on the kitchen door that reads "Well-behaved women rarely make history." A conspicuous chunk of her staff is female (and non-Italian).

"When I had the kids,"—she has twins, two action-packed sons—"I thought: 'Oh, this is what the feminist movement is about.' Going back to work after giving birth felt like a vacation. This idea that women couldn't handle this job because it's physically demanding is total bullshit. It's demanding, but it penalizes anybody who wants to have a family or a normal life. There is no way the female body is not strong enough for this: we already do seventy-five times more things than men."

Erba Brusca is a happy anomaly on the Milanese restaurant scene. It's a bit peripheral and it's always been quietly popular, though never the hottest table in town. Those who know come here for something honest and delicious. The restaurant resembles a greenhouse, with sage-green walls, red steel factory-style window-pane doors, and two patios with creaking wooden floors.

The décor is equal parts industrial and country-sleek—lots of new wood, black and white photos, shelves stacked with wine bottles (Danilo is a sommelier), and cookbooks. Light floods in from the main road, which runs along the Naviglio Pavese, and from the green backyard, where the river Lambro, reduced to a slow stream, bends and softly trickles away. "Danilo saw this place as he was driving by; it used to be called Osteria del Tubetto, this super storico place"—Alice speaks in a delightful Italian-American patois—"with live music, communists, anarchists: it was a ritrovo, their gathering place. When we moved in, there were dishes for cat food and bottles of mosquito repellent everywhere." They liked the idea of bringing back life to a neglected area of Milan. The Milanese love to leave the city on weekends to go to the country, but they forget that the line between city and country used to be very blurry here. "The idea was to say, look, we're in a place that's not perfectly metropolitan or bucolic, but we can grow things and build honest relationships with smaller local producers that are relatively unknown."

Alice has no conventional culinary training. Born in France, she grew up in North Carolina. One of her uncles lived in Italy: she visited him and got her first taste of espresso and her first notions of Italian cuisine. She retained a love for our food but thought of it as a hobby. She majored in political science and Italian literature at Smith College, in Northampton, Massachusetts, and while in school went to Florence on an exchange program. She lived in New York for a while and while working at a law firm she'd go to an Italian restaurant to help make the fresh pasta. A few years later she moved to Milan, following her then-boyfriend. When her plan of starting a legal internship took longer than expected, she fell back on food.

Starting late in the game gave her an advantage: a huge drive to learn. In 2004, she began working at the Park Hyatt hotel, a year and a half later she left to go to The River Café, in London. It was there, working alongside the two legends Ruth Rogers and Rose Grey that she had her epiphany, learning an attention to product she had not seen anywhere else—not even in Italy. "It used to be that the more exotic the product, the better, even though it was frozen or not great quality. Instead, at River Café it was like, 'Italy has the most amazing products in the world, why don't we just put some olive oil on it and call it a day?'" She was inspired by the way the kitchen was organized, seeing how all waiters were asked to partake in prepping, picking herbs, peeling garlic, washing lettuce: they were handling the food and could name all the different vegetables.

Eventually she moved back to Milan, working first at Il Liberty, with Andrea Provenzani, then at Alice, with Viviana Varese. At Alice she understood she had it in her to become executive chef. At Liberty she learned how to make risotto. "I once met an Australian chef who said 'Italian cuisine is so easy even an ox could make it' and I remember thinking, really? I felt so proud of myself when after five years I finally was able to make a perfect risotto. I worked so hard and read so much about it."

A friend introduced her to chef Cesare Battisti and Danilo Ingannamorte, co-founders of Ratanà. Cesare was already one of the key figures of the city's gastronomic renaissance, a serious connoisseur of Lombardy's traditions and products. (Ratanà was the first neo-trattoria in Milan and while it may not be on the "ones to watch" list anymore, it's a staple, and incredibly formative for those who pass through it.) In 2010, the three decided to open Erba Brusca ("sorrel"). Ever since the first service, emphasis has been on vegetables, though fish and meat are served too, all sourced from sustainable cooperatives and farms. "It's taken us eight years to get to the point where we're really growing produce for us." To do this, Danilo and Alice recently bought a piece of land a few hundred feet from the restaurant and established a fully functioning urban farm. One acre is planted with "all kind of *ortaggi*": tomatoes, zucchini, arugula, lettuce, chicory, cucumbers, eggplants, fennel, carrots, leeks, onions, kale, beets, celeriac, mustard, pumpkins, cabbages, sorrel, nasturtium, mint, thyme, basil, strawberries, melons, and watermelons. Danilo maintains it with the help of a young gardener and his two sons, who can often be found watering the plants, oblivious to the dirt and the sting of the occasional bee.

Alice and Danilo are not "zero food mile" fanatics. They believe sustainability can't outweigh taste. Sometimes, a lower carbon footprint doesn't mean better flavor. "Plus, if a small producer uses his car to bring you the food every day, how are you offsetting the carbon footprint?" What does matter to Alice and Danilo is seasonality. She urges me to take home some zucchini. "They come up in twenty-four hours! It's like when in the winter people come in and go, 'ci sono solo cavoli,' all you're serving is cabbages, and I'll be like, 'I know— but lots of different kinds of cavoli!'" This overabundance has lead to a distinctive style of dish building, which has come to be considered "very Erba Brusca." In many ways, it recalls The River Café, as well as Canal House and Chez Panisse. "We tend to layer the same vegetables in the same dish because we have a lot of all of them. For instance, we'll do a base of chickpea hummus and then layer grilled zucchini and a salad of raw julienned zucchini and then pumpkin seeds and zucchini blossoms. Or we'll do roasted pumpkin, a pumpkin cream, and raw butternut squash marinated with vinegar and oregano."

Alice's food is conclusively, absolutely Italian, with a few foreign touches that feel sensible and sexy. "Italian food is the food that really inspired me to cook. It's the most exciting to me. But the cool thing is I didn't grow up here, so I don't go "oh, this tastes like my nonna's food." I had a nonna who cooked, but she was English: Yorkshire pudding is what reminds me of my childhood. I don't have all that ingrained tradition and I'm not shackled. I feel Italians have struggled that way in finding their voice: you can't add mint to parmigiana di melanzane, that sort of thing."

Alice doesn't do rivisitazioni but there are some things she draws from around the world, particularly the Mediterranean basin, things that can be found in Sicily as well as in North Africa, some spices and techniques. "I'm not trying to shock and awe; I'm still learning as I go. Take fermentation: we're not all Noma, we can't all ferment squid ink and think it's delicious. At Erba Brusca we ferment things like cucumbers, which makes them spicier."

She points out the importance of considering the flavor property of each ingredient before adding it to a dish. Take her risotto (page 71): Alice will go through over twenty pounds of Carnaroli rice per service, even in the summer. She likes risotto because its creamy texture allows it to hold its own even with fermented or spicy elements, which she likes to use to finish.

From her privileged observation point—an outsider with an inside track—she has seen non-Italians, particularly Americans, become very curious about all Italian food, willing to learn more about it beyond the usual places (Rome, Naples, Sicily). Foreigners, she says, are now seeing Italian cooking as an elevated art form, the same way they've been used to seeing French cuisine. "They're willing to spend money on it, to trust the chef, and learn about it." According to Alice, the most problematic customers are Italians: "They seem to be suffering from a nonna complex, still. You don't see that many people who are not in the business order tasting menus: they like to choose, to have control. French customers, on the other hand, revere the cook: they go to a restaurant to eat better than at home."

As we sit on Erba Brusca's back porch, listening to the Lambro's persistent murmur, and the rustling of ivy in the evening air, I ask Alice to pick one word to define Italian cuisine. "I just had a friend over from Copenhagen. He works at Manfreds, where they make some of my favorite food in the world. He said of his meal here, 'There's something, a quality I can't put my finger on, but it's what I miss when I'm not in Italy.' After a while he figured the right term was goloso." Goloso, which doesn't necessarily mean rich or fatty, can be used to describe very elevated dishes as well as lowly ones, and has something to do with comfort, and deliciousness, and balance. Something elusive. Goloso: untranslatable. But you get the gist.

Risotto con Robiola, Limone e Paprika Affumicata
Risotto with Creamy Cheese, Preserved Lemon, and Smoked Paprika

Alice Delcourt uses preserved lemons, a Moroccan specialty, to brighten up this creamy risotto. While she makes her own by pickling quartered lemons in brine for one month, you can find jars of preserved lemons in specialty food stores. By pairing the velvety, round-tasting risotto base with piquant finishing elements, Alice adds a kick to a great classic.

5-7 cups chicken broth
1 tablespoon extra virgin olive oil
1 shallot, peeled and diced
2 cups Carnaroli rice
3 tablespoon unsalted butter
¼ cup finely grated Parmigiano Reggiano cheese
4 oz. Robiola cheese (you may substitute with a fresh, mild goat cheese)
Half of a preserved lemon (only the rind, finely diced)
1 teaspoon smoked paprika

Serves 4

Heat the chicken broth in a medium saucepan over medium heat; adjust flame to maintain a slow simmer. Heat olive oil in a heavy, wide saucepan over medium heat. When oil is hot, add diced shallot and sauté until translucent. Add the rice and cook, stirring constantly, until glassy and too hot to hold in your hand, 3 to 4 minutes. Stir in a ladleful of warm broth and cook, stirring often, until broth is mostly absorbed, about 2 to 3 minutes. Continue adding broth, one ladleful at a time, stirring until absorbed. Adjust heat between medium or medium-low to keep the risotto barely simmering. Cook, stirring often, until rice is just tender but still al dente (not mushy). The risotto should have the consistency of a creamy porridge, but should not be soupy. Remove from heat, add butter, Parmigiano Reggiano, Robiola, and lemon rind; stir until creamy and well combined.

Divide between 4 warm serving plates, sprinkle with smoked paprika, and serve immediately.

LUCA
GRASSELLI

We're driving through La Bassa, the lowlands of Pianura Padana surrounding the river Po, flat farming land, mostly clayey, often cloaked in mist. Sleepy towns roll by with their red brick country churches, grocery shops and bars, and the villas, a bit rundown under the ivy, where the old-money families of Cremona have been coming for generations; herons fly over the cascine, the farmhouses that used to make up the spinal cord of this land and are now reduced to just a few functioning ones.

We're heading to a cascina dating back to the seventeenth century. It gets its name from a pond where, according to legend, plague victims used to be buried. (Lagoscuro means "dark lake".) The name is haunting, but Lagoscuro is a nothing short of a fairy tale, fit for a memorable egg-hunt, for a summer staging of *Finding Neverland*, for a dream wedding, for a new life. The main house, with its crenellated walls and tower, overlooks an immense courtyard and is flanked by two long buildings, one serving as living quarters for the owners, one as farming shed and barn. It's the typical u-shaped structure of the cascine, designed by the necessity to have everything within viewing and walking distance, and to create a protected enclosure for chickens, geese, rabbits, and the other *animali da cortile* (courtyard animals). The back of the main building opens out onto a verdant expanse where getting lost is easy. Cow stables, a pigsty, a dairy, a couple of empty barns (painted floor to ceiling by a group of artists during a summer residency), another barn filled with antique furniture and old farming tools, guarded by black and white photographs in oval frames. Wandering, we run into a free-roaming turkey and a peacock, while the only humans in sight are bent over the plots, picking vegetables. A path unfurls into the woods leading to the lake's shore. We catch glimpses of the dark water through the willows that follow its edge like embroidery on a napkin's edge.

Lagoscuro is run by Luca Grasselli, a descendant of the original owners. Young and dynamic, with a strawberry-blond mop of curls and a freckled, friendly face, he lives in one of the wings of the cascina with his wife Federica and their children, while the young staff occupies a handful of upstairs rooms in the main building.

The main building's ground floor is organized around a central hallway that connects front and back, so that a glimpse of the garden is the first thing you see as soon as you walk in. There are frescoed ceilings, their colors faded, chandeliers, stained mirrors, antique tables, and mismatched chairs. Sitting rooms and dining rooms, large and small, corridors, and staircases giving into more rooms with cupboards full of crisp, old linens and enough dinnerware to supply an army.

Luca calls Lagoscuro a *cascina biologica multifunzionale*. "We're farmers and we're hosts: we sell what we grow, the cheese we make, the meats from our animals, our jars of pickles and preserves, and we also serve them to the people who come eat our fixed-course menus on weekends." I ask him which plates he's going to use for the dishes we're going to photograph. He shows me a minimalist Scandinavian-style set he commissioned from a local artisan. I ask him if we can use some of his family's ceramics instead. He opens a few drawers. "Pick anything you want." There are Italian, French, English, and Japanese pieces, some hand-painted, some antique, a few that seem of quite considerable value; there are botanical motifs, rural scenes, abstract patterns. There are at least forty tureens, and one is decorated with the Grasselli family crest. It's a treasure hunt.

The first Grassellis to settle in the cascina, centuries ago, were wealthy scholars who maintained a palazzo in Cremona and would go to the country to escape the heat and read. The house was passed down all the way to Luca's father's uncle, who established his residence there with his wife. "But it was too big for just the two of them, so they offered it to my dad and his brother. Eventually it became my parents' house, and pretty soon they started hosting big dinners for a few guests, mostly friends. Then word spread, my father built a proper kitchen and it became a cucina in cascina operation."

After a while, Fabio Grasselli, who mostly goes by "nonno" (even his son Luca calls him that), grew bored. A former student of medicine, he bought a cheesemaking manual and started experimenting. He then ordered his first cows and reserved a vast area for their pasture, so as to never have too many heads of cattle per hectare and to continuously move them from field to field. "Now we make twelve kinds of cheese, plus yogurt, and every day we go through two hundred liters of our own organic raw milk."

Mozzarella, ricotta, provola, latteria, formaggella, taleggio, erborinato, robiola: soft and hard, young and seasoned, raw curd, semi-cooked curd, pulled curd and blue, washed rind, cow's and goat's. You name it, they have it. Luca's dad has been selling his cheese to restaurants and specialized markets for twenty years, building quite a reputation for himself, even with the notoriously difficult crowd at French cheese fairs. In his mid-sixties, he's as handsome and fit as his son, with immaculate white hair worn under a crochet hat, and skin tanned from working in the fields.

He walks past us on his way to the cellar, where he's about to check on his cheese. "Ciao nonno!" Luca calls out, and then whispers to me, "he's the hardest-working of us all."

Luca has a graduate degree in philosophy (he specialized in "history of ideas," with a dissertation on urban-rural linkages), and a master's degree from Università di Scienze Gastronomiche in Pollenzo. When he

took over from his dad he knew he wanted to push a bit harder. "I already loved the hospitality industry, but I knew in order to be sustainable we had to do many different things, not just one. So I borrowed some money to remodel the kitchen, and I planted two hectares with organic vegetables. We started making bread, reserved a space for the production of sauces and jarred goods, and my wife opened a kindergarten, catering to the local community. The idea initially was to sell these products at the shop we have in Cremona and through farmers' markets, but now we supply a few restaurants as well. We work only with like-minded people, such as Alice and Danilo from Erba Brusca" (see page 64).

Lagoscuro operates as a restaurant on weekends: the rest of the time it can be booked for events, weddings, parties, dinners with guest chefs, or wine tastings, usually involving small producers of biodynamic wines, a community that seems to gravitate naturally around places like this. "This farmhouse is like an old elephant: it takes a while to get it up and walking, and once you've started it up you have to keep nudging it. When I took over, it was just me in the kitchen, with Federica managing the front of house and my dad helping with cheese and charcuterie. We never advertised what we did but slowly we have grown." The kitchen is constantly bustling now, as Luca can count on a tight group of energetic youngsters. They've come here entranced by the rural mystique and in turn they have found so much more: this is a 360-degree life experience. Recipes are written on the tiled walls, music is blasting. There's a sense of organized chaos, which seems to be the way everything is done here.

"We're so busy we rarely have time to travel, but the cool thing is the world comes to us, to teach and learn. We had a group of guys from restaurant Septime, in Paris: they stayed for three months. There's an Italian guy who used to work in a circus in Barcelona: he's in charge of pizza and focaccia. One of our guys interned with Magnus Nilsson, at Fäviken, and there's an Italian chef from Copenhagen with his girlfriend, he used to work with Christian Puglisi, she with Richard Hart. People are always coming and going."

As I explore the kitchen, Luca starts shaping bread. "We grow our own grains, an evolutionary population of wheat, einkorn and rye, all stone-milled locally. We make one type of bread with an einkorn polenta and seeds, and one with sprouted einkorn." We taste the bread and some delicious *grissini* (breadsticks) with our antipasti spread: the farm's own cheese and charcuterie, pickles and vegetables packed in oil, a huge salad, lettuce and Chioggia beets, with their pink and white rings, still warm from the garden. The courses keep coming: a vegetable risotto (recipe on page 79); two kinds of fresh ravioli: one filled with ricotta and borage, dressed with lemon-scented butter and dill flowers, the other with blue cheese and roasted cherry tomatoes; braised beef with sautéed potatoes and red cabbage; dessert is a fruit tart (recipe on page 81), classic and fresh.

It's simple Italian farm food, designed to showcase what's produced either on the farm or locally. Luca uses no pyrotechnics: he cooks hearty and delicious dishes, with solid technique and little tweaks on tradition that make everything more sensible, nutritious, sustainable. The risotto is topped with roasted vegetable scraps, left over from the production of the house giardiniera, and a vegetable jus to replace the classic meat-based fondo bruno; or the tart crust, made with the farm's einkorn flour.

The menu at Cascina Lagoscuro is prix fixe: thirty-three Euros will buy you antipasti, two first courses, a second course with a vegetable side, and three desserts. Wine is extra, but coffee and amari are on the house. Luca says he sometimes feels like he's tilting at windmills: some people complain his menu is too expensive, which is ridiculous considering how much food he serves, and the quality of the ingredients he uses, not to mention the amount of work that goes into each dish. He's thinking of slowly shifting to a family-style format, more focused on the antipasti, with just one main dish and dessert. "I want our menu to tell the story of who we are and what we do, and I also want to make the workload a little lighter on us. I would like to keep growing, but I also intend to keep this a family operation. This will never be a hotel, nor a five-days-a-week restaurant."

As he's thinking of ways to make the operation more productive—weddings are still the main source of income—he's toying with the idea of fixing up one of the barns to turn it into a wine bar with a small food menu. But building a network of like-minded young farmers is his fondest dream. It might take some time. "It makes me sad to see all those decrepit cascine around here, next to the intensive cow farms. Lagoscuro is a bit of an anomaly and we've been quite isolated because of this. We need to step out of this isolation and find more people like us. Though I know building something like this from scratch is a massive undertaking! I was born into this place. Sometimes I can't believe my own luck."

78

Risotto al Fondo Bruno Vegetale
Risotto with Vegetable Gravy

This vegetable gravy is intended as a way to recycle vegetable scraps from a commercial kitchen. Any leftover vegetables will do: carrot tops, onion skins, beet greens, zucchini stems, cauliflower or broccoli stalks, celery—whatever is on hand. Because it's rare to find three lbs. of vegetable scraps laying around a home kitchen, feel free to use whole or sliced seasonal vegetables as well. You can find kudzu root starch, a Japanese thickening agent, in organic/health food stores, and online.

Risotto
5–7 cups homemade or store-bought vegetable broth
3 tablespoons extra-virgin olive oil
2 cups Arborio or Carnaroli rice
1 cup dry white wine
4 tablespoons butter, cut into chunks
¾ cup grated Parmigiano Reggiano cheese
Salt, to taste

To finish
1 cup finely chopped, mixed grilled vegetables (such as zucchini, eggplant, carrot, onion)
Vegetable gravy (recipe follows)

Serves 4

For the risotto
Heat the vegetable broth in a medium saucepan over medium heat; adjust flame to maintain a slow simmer. Heat olive oil in a heavy, wide saucepan over medium heat. When oil is hot, add the rice and cook, stirring constantly, until somewhat translucent, 3 to 4 minutes. Pour in the wine and cook until absorbed, 1 to 2 minutes. Stir in a ladleful of warm vegetable broth and cook, stirring often, until broth is mostly absorbed, 2 to 3 minutes. Continue adding broth, one ladleful at a time, and stirring until absorbed. Adjust heat to keep the risotto barely simmering (between medium and medium-low). Cook, stirring often, until rice is just tender but still al dente (not mushy). Remove from heat, add butter, Parmigiano, and salt to taste; stir to combine.

To finish
Divide the risotto among 4 warm serving plates; garnish with a spoonful of vegetable gravy and chopped, grilled vegetables.

Vegetable Gravy
3 lbs. vegetable scraps or sliced vegetables (like carrots, celery, cauliflower, broccoli, zucchini, eggplant, onions, garlic, etc.)
¼ cup extra-virgin olive oil
2 tablespoons tomato paste
4 cups plus 2 teaspoons water, divided
1 sheet dried kombu seaweed
2 teaspoons kuzu root starch
½ teaspoon salt, or more to taste

Preheat the oven to 325°F. Spread the vegetable scraps in an even layer on two rimmed baking sheets. Place in preheated oven and bake for 20 minutes. Remove the pans from the oven, add 2 tablespoons of olive oil and 1 tablespoon of tomato paste to each pan and toss to coat. Return pans to oven and cook for another 20 minutes, until vegetables are soft and beginning to brown. Carefully pour 2 cups of water (or enough to just cover the vegetables) in each pan. Continue to cook for 40 minutes.

Carefully remove pans from the oven. Pour the liquid through a fine mesh strainer and into a medium saucepan, discarding vegetable solids. Place saucepan over medium-high heat and bring to a steady boil; cook until the broth has reduced by half, about 30 minutes. Reduce to a simmer, add kombu to the saucepan and cook for 5 minutes. In a small dish, stir together kuzu root starch and 2 teaspoons of cold water until smooth, and then whisk the paste into the simmering vegetable stock. Cook, whisking constantly, until thickened, 2 to 3 minutes. Add salt, remove from heat, and keep warm until ready to use.

Crostata di Frutta al Monococco
Fruit Tart with Einkorn Crust

Fresh fruit is the real star of this show-stopping dessert, while a thin layer of gluten-free pastry cream binds it all together. Make sure to buy the freshest seasonal fruit and feel free to make substitutions depending on what's at its peak. Whole wheat einkorn flour has a weak gluten and ensures a nuttier, more rustic texture.

Crust

1 stick plus 1 tablespoon unsalted butter (4.5 oz.), softened
⅔ cup granulated sugar (4.5 oz.)
½ teaspoon finely grated lemon zest
seeds from ½ vanilla bean (reserve pod for pastry cream)
1 large egg
2 cups and 1 tablespoon (9 oz.) whole wheat einkorn flour
½ teaspoon baking powder
¼ teaspoon salt

Pastry Cream

1 cup whole milk
½ vanilla bean pod, emptied of seeds (see above)
⅓ cup granulated sugar
3 medium egg yolks
1 small pinch of salt
¼ cup cornstarch
2 tablespoons unsalted butter cut into pieces, at room temperature

Tart

1 ½ lbs. fresh, sliced, seasonal fruit and berries (eg: 5 apricots, ½ apple, 2 cups mixed berries)

Serves 6

Prepare the crust: Combine the butter, sugar, vanilla seeds, and lemon zest in the bowl of a stand mixer fitted with a paddle attachment. Mix on medium speed until combined, 2 to 3 minutes. Scrape down sides of bowl, add egg, mix thoroughly and scrape down sides of bowl again.

In a medium bowl, stir together flour, baking powder, and salt. Slowly pour dry ingredients to the butter-egg mixture, and mix on medium speed for 2 minutes. Turn the dough onto a sheet of plastic wrap and press into a 6-inch disk, wrapping tightly. Refrigerate for at least 12 hours, and up to 2 days.

Preheat oven to 350°F. Butter a 9-inch tart pan or spray with nonstick cooking spray; set aside.

Remove the dough from the refrigerator and bring to room temperature. Roll out on a lightly floured surface to a 13-inch round, about ¼-inch thick. (Dough will be fragile, but don't worry if it falls apart, you can always patch up broken spots directly in the pan.) Carefully transfer to prepared pan and press gently to adhere. Using a sharp knife, trim dough flush with pan. Patch any cracks with dough scraps. Line the crust with a round of parchment paper and fill with pie weights or dried beans. Bake in preheated oven for 9 minutes, remove pie weights and parchment, prick holes in the bottom of the crust with a fork, and bake until golden and fragrant, another 5-6 minutes. Remove from oven and set aside on a wire rack to cool.

Prepare the pastry cream: Pour milk into a small saucepan, add the vanilla pod and warm over low heat until just steaming; do not boil. Meanwhile, in the bowl of a stand mixer fitted with a whisk attachment (or with a hand mixer), whisk together sugar and egg yolks on medium-low speed until smooth and pale, about 2-3 minutes. Add salt and corn starch; mix on low speed for 2 minutes, scraping down sides of bowl when necessary. With the mixer on low speed, slowly pour in the hot milk and vanilla pod, until thoroughly combined. (Tip: you may want to transfer the milk from the saucepan to a pitcher or spouted measuring cup, to make pouring easier.)

Pour the pastry cream through a fine mesh sieve into a clean, medium-sized saucepan; discard solids and vanilla pod. Cook over low heat, whisking constantly, until the mixture thickens and begins to barely simmer, about 8 minutes. Remove from heat, stir in butter. Continue whisking until completely smooth.

Fill a large bowl with ice water, set aside. Pour the pastry cream into a heatproof bowl and set over ice bath. Stir occasionally until cooled to room temperature. Cover tightly with plastic wrap and transfer to refrigerator until ready to use. (The pastry cream will last in the refrigerator for up to two days.)

To serve

When the crust and pastry cream are both completely cooled, transfer the crust to a serving plate, spread pastry cream over the bottom and refrigerate until set, about 1 hour. Meanwhile, wash and slice fruit as desired. When the filling is set, arrange fruit on top. Serve immediately, or chill (for no longer than three hours) until ready to serve.

DAMIANO

DONATI

Damiano Donati is a handsome devil: he's got the looks and the tail to prove it. He carries around quite a lot of ink, one arm fully tattooed with Japanese motifs, one with a slaughtered pig and a bunch of vegetables. Hidden under his clothes is a bona fide devil's tail in ink, stretching from his butt all the way down to his heel. I didn't see it with my own eyes but Stefano Manias of Al Cjasal (see page 216) who interned at three-Michelin-starred Le Calandre with Damiano and shared a house with him, described it to me in full detail.

Given this look, it would be easy to dismiss this young lucchese as just another "bad boy chef," but that would be a gross misjudgment of character: Donati is one of the most genuine and profound people I know. He also happens to make some of the best bread I've ever had. He's a self-taught baker and was attracted, as many bakers are, not by bread per se, but by fermentation, the challenge of managing something that is alive and unpredictable. On this path he was assisted by Gabriele Bonci, a celebrity in the world of pizza romana lovers. They met during an olive oil event, and started exchanging photos of their doughs, tips, and ideas (it was following Bonci's suggestion that Damiano developed his guinea fowl, which is marinated in creamy sourdough starter and then fried: recipe on page 89). Bread, along with spaghetti al pomodoro, is the litmus test I use to gauge a chef's true skills and attitude. In the case of Damiano, it proves he's an agriculture nerd (he bakes with local grains, like Verna, an old variety of bread wheat, working closely with farmers and millers), and extremely ingenious. A few years back, while he was first trying to make panettone, he modified a chest freezer so it could work as a retarder-proofer (an appliance that can be programmed to follow specific temperature and humidity cycles). "I was afraid it would short and set the kitchen on fire so I slept by it, on a cot. It went on for days. It never caught fire, but it never really worked, either."

Ingenuity and manual dexterity both run in his family. "My grandpa was a great plumber, my uncle is a well-known vintage motorcycle restorer. My mom is a beautician, my dad is a bus driver who is also a pretty good home cook. I have always made stuff with my hands—I paint, I build furniture with driftwood. Growing up, I knew I'd either be a mechanic or a cook."

He started picking up busboy shifts at restaurants on weekends when he was fourteen. He then went to catering school but eventually dropped out. A few restaurants later, he interned at Le Calandre, then started working at Serendepico, a country-chic resort on the hills outside Lucca. The quality of his food made him a media darling and earned him several prestigious awards. And then he quit.

Damiano took a sabbatical, and it's fair to say he went a little wild and a little mad—a life-shaping experience that eventually formed the bedrock for what has followed. For a year, he lived at La Cerreta, a farming commune near Livorno. "Over there, if you wanted a chicken, you had to kill it yourself; if you wanted pork, you had to slaughter a pig; if you wanted milk, you had to milk a cow," he recalls. The extreme sort of existence at La Cerreta helped him home in on what mattered to him: truth, the sometimes ruthless law of the land, and a certain attitude he calls "elegant brutality"—the motto of what would later become Punto Officina del Gusto, the restaurant next to the famous Piazza dell'Anfiteatro (imagine the piazza from Siena's palio horse race, but on a miniature scale) which for about six years (it closed in 2020) represented one of the better executed versions of neo-trattoria I've tried. Punto, as the place's full name suggested, was an officina, an aptly chosen term that signifies both "mechanic's shop" and "artisan's lab." Each day ideas and ingredients were taken apart and put back together; it was a makers' shop, with a palpable energy.

After starting his tenure there, Damiano had flown to Paris to spend a short break at Iñaki Aizpitarte's Le Chateaubriand, one of the most incisive neo-bistros, a shattering novelty when it first opened, and deliciously irreverent still. Iñaki changes his menu every day and tends to not write down recipes. Damiano is the same way. (This may be inevitable when working under the constraints of à la minute cooking, but it presents a problem: how can you codify something as significant as the trattoria or the bistro if you don't write anything down? Can the survival of this "species" rely solely on oral transmission? Should trattoria even be taught? Maybe you can't really teach how to build or work a trattoria, but you can create a trattoria culture, so that more and more young chefs will want to open one.)

As a result, Damiano doesn't really like to talk about his process, unless one presses. Take his sliced turkey roast. "I really wanted to do something with turkey because I don't think there's a more mistreated, dumbed-down meat in Italian cuisine. I was also thinking of things like scaloppine and sliced roasts, those dishes you'd eat at a very classic hotel's restaurant while on vacation on the Riviera with your family, dressed with a nice *fondo slegato*." (A *fondo slegato*, literally "unbound jus," also known as *intingolo* or *salsa splittata*, is a cornerstone of Italian cuisine, a favorite of chefs like Paolo Lopriore, Niko Romito, and Davide Caranchini.) There's much uncomplicated flavor in this sauce of olive oil and tomato, or olive oil and vinegar or broth, with fresh herbs, onions or garlic, maybe capers or olives too, and sometimes the drippings of cooked meat, fish, and vegetables, deglazed simply with a little wine or lemon juice. It's not smooth, it's not glossy. It's a bomb. What's more Italian than that?

Damiano's fondi slegati and dishes like tortelli with cream, ham, and peas (a sophisticated take on a 1980s classic), or spaghetti with butter and fermented plums, or the Chicken and Vegetable Aspic served with Giardiniera (recipe on page 91) are signs of a contemporary mind at work on elements of our culinary identity: "I have been thinking about building a menu based on i *gesti*," [literally 'the gestures,' or

'movements'] della cucina italiana. Elements of foreign cuisines are seeping into the fabric of our dishes and while I think it can be interesting I also think we still have so much to say and very little to envy in the world."

In Damiano's personal system of beliefs this concept of what it means to be an Italian cook has always been indissoluble from having an almost primal connection to the land. So it makes sense that following Punto, he would go back to it. In June 2020 he kicked off "Fuoco e Materia" (fire and matter), a chef's table series hosted by Azienda Agricola Sardi, a farm with hospitality on the hills just outside Lucca, owned by the Sardi Giustiniani family. (Jacopo Giustiniani is affiliated with the SA Hospitality Group, which run the Sant'Ambroeus restaurants and Felice wine bars in the States).

"The property sits in the middle of fifty acres of farming land, with biodynamic vineyards, orchards, wheat, and legumes fields. I started collaborating with them while still at Punto, and establishing my new base there was quite the natural evolution."

One of the first orders of business of his new tenure was building a Georgian oven (similar to a tandoor), where he plans on making flatbreads. He has also had a local blacksmith build him a special grilling setup, with several stations of his own design. As this book is preparing to go to press he's planning on cooking most of his dishes with fire, serving breads baked in a woodfired oven and a tight selection of biodynamic wines (for which the Lucchesia is becoming a new mecca) and ciders—naturally, Damiano makes his own.

"I'm going to build a very visceral cuisine," he says. "I'm closing a circle."

Faraona Marinata nel Lievito Madre e Fritta
Starter-Marinated and Fried Guinea Fowl

Damiano got the idea for the dish from Roman pizza master Gabriele Bonci, of Pizzarium. In his version Bonci refreshes the starter marinade every day. Because Damiano's cuisine is more acidity-driven he lets the guinea fowl sit in the same starter for seven to ten days, in order to reach the point where lactic fermentation gives way to acidic fermentation. This not only tenderizes the meat but also adds one extra layer of depth to its flavor.

4 whole guinea fowl legs, complete with thigh, drumstick, and foot
4 cups creamy sourdough starter
1 small red onion
½ cup plus 2 teaspoons red wine vinegar, divided
2 small beets
5 cups canola oil, for frying
3 cups shredded lettuce
1 tablespoon extra virgin olive oil
salt and pepper

Place the guinea fowl legs in a large plastic container and toss with the starter, making sure the meat is completely submerged. Cover and place in the refrigerator to marinate for 7 to 10 days.

The day before cooking, slice the onion into thin disks and place in shallow bowl or non-reactive container. Add ½ cup of the vinegar, cover, and refrigerate overnight. Drain and pat dry before serving.

Preheat oven to 400°F. Scrub the beets and wrap each one in a sheet of aluminum foil. Bake in preheated oven until beets are tender when poked with a fork, about 45 minutes. Place the beets, still wrapped in aluminum foil, in a plastic container or bowl. Let cool at room temperature for 1 hour. Unwrap the beets and collect their juices in a small bowl. Save the beets for another use. Set aside beet juice.

Remove the guinea fowl from the refrigerator and let sit at room temperature for 1 hour. Meanwhile, heat the canola oil in a large Dutch oven or wok until a cube of bread sizzles when tossed into the hot oil. Working in two batches, remove guinea fowl legs from the starter and gently submerge in the hot oil. Fry for 12 to 13 minutes, turning gently after about 6 minutes. Transfer to a wire rack to drain, tent with aluminum foil and let rest for 5 to 7 minutes before serving.

Place the shredded lettuce in a medium bowl, add 1 tablespoon of beet juice, olive oil, 2 teaspoons red wine vinegar, salt, and pepper to taste. Toss to combine.

Place 1 guinea fowl leg on each of 4 serving plates. Garnish with salad and marinated onions. Serve immediately.

Not to be mistaken for *galantina di pollo* (a deboned chicken filled with a forcemeat of ground pork and veal, lard, tongue, and other ingredients, which is cooked and coated in a thin layer of gelatin), this aspic has an almost 1:1 ratio of gelatin and filling. Aspics were particularly in vogue in the eighties and nineties and were featured on many Italian tables at Christmas. Young chefs are rediscovering their appeal: versatility, freshness, and elegance. Damiano serves his aspic with a homemade umeboshi paste—his takes a whole year to make but you can get yours at specialty stores and Japanese markets.

3 boneless chicken breasts
Salt
3 small zucchini, cut into 4 to 6 spears
10 asparagus stalks, trimmed
15 green beans, trimmed
2 ¼ cups clarified chicken broth (recipe follows)
10 sheets leaf gelatin
10 giardiniera-brined onions (recipe follows)
10 giardiniera-brined carrots (recipe follows)
50 grams umeboshi paste, see above
Extra virgin olive oil
Pepper

Serves 4

Cut each chicken breast into 7 to 8 long strips. Bring a medium pot of water to boil over high heat. When boiling, add a tablespoon of salt and the chicken pieces; reduce to medium heat and cook at a steady simmer for 8 to 9 minutes. Remove chicken with a slotted spoon and set aside to cool.

Add the zucchini spears, asparagus stalks, and green beans to the water; bring back to a boil and cook for 3 minutes. Strain and set aside.

In a rectangular dish, such as a 4 x 9-inch loaf pan or other non-reactive container, arrange the chicken strips and vegetables snugly in alternating rows, to distribute the colors and flavors evenly.

Place the gelatin sheets in a shallow dish and cover with cold water; set aside for 10 minutes.

Meanwhile, heat the clarified chicken broth in a small saucepan over medium heat until steaming but not boiling. Remove from heat. Lift gelatin sheets with a slotted spoon, squeezing gently to wring out excess water. Gently add gelatin to the warm broth, stirring to combine until completely dissolved. Slowly pour the mixture into the pan, completely submerging the chicken and vegetables. Tap the pan gently a few times to remove any air bubbles. Set aside to cool at room temperature for 1 hour, and then refrigerate overnight.

Remove pan from refrigerator and cover with a cutting board; invert quickly. Tap the pan gently to loosen the aspic onto the board. Cut

Pollo in Gelatina + Giardiniera
Chicken and Vegetable Aspic + Giardiniera

the aspic into 1-inch slices. Place each slice on a plate; drizzle with olive oil, season with freshly ground black pepper and garnish with giardiniera vegetables and umeboshi paste.

Clarified Chicken Broth
3 lbs. uncooked chicken parts (such as a whole, cut-up chicken; or wings, legs, necks, backs, and trimmings)
3 carrots
3 celery stalks
1 red onion, peeled and halved
1 tomato, quartered
16 whole cloves
2 three-inch segments of cinnamon sticks, divided
Salt and pepper to taste
1 yellow onion, peeled
2 boneless chicken breasts
1 cup dry white wine
5 egg whites
1 rind of Parmigiano Reggiano

Place chicken parts in a large stockpot and cover with 12 cups cold water. Coarsely chop 2 carrots and 2 celery stalks, and add to the stockpot along with red onion, tomato, 8 cloves, 1 cinnamon stick, and 1 tablespoon of salt. Bring to a simmer over medium-low heat, skimming foam off the top as it forms, for about 30 minutes. Cook at a slow simmer for 3 to 4 hours. Strain broth through a fine mesh sieve and set aside to cool completely at room temperature, about 2 hours.

Very finely dice remaining carrot, celery stalk, yellow onion, and chicken breasts and combine in a large pot. Add remaining 8 cloves, cinnamon stick, white wine, egg whites, Parmigiano Reggiano rind, and cooled chicken broth. Place over low heat and bring to a slow boil, stirring frequently. Reduce heat and simmer for 10 minutes; remove from heat. Let cool for 2 hours at room temperature then filter with a fine mesh sieve into a bowl.

Giardiniera
Damiano Donati is not the only chef in the book who makes his own giardiniera; this preparation is originally Piedmontese, so it won't come as a surprise that Turin's Banco (see page 230) serves one made with both vegetables and fruits (cherries and apricots). In Tuscany, Damiano also makes this simple, vegetable-only version to accompany his chicken aspic. Feel free to vary the vegetables based on the season and varieties available locally; bell peppers, zucchini, squash and green beans are popular additions. The total amount of trimmed, raw vegetables should add up to 2 lbs. Save your scraps to make the Fondo Vegetale (Vegetable Gravy) on page 79.

For the brine:
6 1/2 cups water
2 cups white wine vinegar
3 tablespoons salt
3 tablespoons sugar
5 garlic cloves, peeled
10 black peppercorns
6 cloves
5 juniper berries
3 fresh or dried bay leaves
1 one-inch segment of cinnamon stick

For the vegetables:
3 cups small cauliflower florets
6 small carrots, cut in half lengthwise
3 celery ribs, cut crosswise into 1-inch pieces
10 radishes, cut in half lengthwise
6 spring onions, cut in half lengthwise

Fill a large bowl with ice water. Combine the brine ingredients in a medium saucepan. Bring to a boil over high heat, and immediately add the cauliflower florets. Cook for 2 minutes, adjusting the heat to maintain a steady simmer, and add the carrots and celery. Continue cooking for 3 minutes, then add the radishes and spring onions, and simmer for a final 3 minutes. Using a slotted spoon, carefully remove the vegetables and garlic from brine and transfer to the ice bath. Strain the hot brine with a fine mesh strainer, discarding spices. Allow brine to cool at room temperature for 1 hour, then transfer to refrigerator until completely cool. Meanwhile, drain the vegetables in a colander and transfer them to a 2-quart jar or other airtight container.

When the brine has cooled completely, pour it over the vegetables, making sure they are submerged. Tightly close the lid, transfer to the refrigerator, and let rest for 2 weeks before serving.

ALESSANDRO MIOCCHI

& GIUSEPPE LO IUDICE

If you manage not to slip on the *sampietrini* (the polished, cube-like basalt stones that make up so much of the pavement in the center of Rome), walking around Retrobottega's neighborhood can be a movie-like experience. Trevi fountain, the Spanish steps, the Pantheon, Ara Pacis, and the river Tiber are all within a few minutes of Via della Stelletta, where the restaurant is located, as are Palazzo Chigi and Montecitorio (the residence of Italy's Prime Minister and the seat of our Chamber of Deputies), with their guarded booths.

History seeps from each crack, scratch, and peeling layer of paint—such is Rome. Take Via del Babuino, where sculptor Antonio Canova maintained one of his studios, or via Margutta, a longtime artists' haven, where Federico Fellini used to live, as did Gregory Peck's character in Roman Holiday. It's an interesting mix of rarefied and humble, of upscale and working class, with precious boutiques wedged between old bakeries and osterie, barber shops caught on the cusp of turning hip, and vintage shop signs that would turn the head of more than one typeface geek. Among the newest signs, and a personal favorite of mine, is the supersized inverted black "R" that signals the entrance to Retrobottega.

The first time I came here, a few years back, Rome was stuck in a gastronomic funk. Alessandro Miocchi and Giuseppe Lo Iudice had just opened the first version of Retrobottega: stools, counters, lots of inexpensive wood and raw metal, a tiny, open-view kitchen, a menu written on a blackboard, changing weekly. Both Miocchi and Lo Iudice had received an impressive training: Miocchi at Crippa's Piazza Duomo and Il Pellicano (a luxury resort on the coast of Tuscany which at the time had two Michelin stars and was helmed by Antonio Guida). He then worked at Il Pagliaccio, in Rome, with Anthony Genovese; there he met Lo Iudice, a business school graduate whose career had taken him from London to New York and then back to Italy. Not long after, they decided to branch out on their own. As a reaction to the more elaborate style of cuisine they were used to, they decided to focus on good and simple offerings, researching exceptional ingredients and transforming them with a sensible use of complex techniques. They were clearly doing something right, because pretty soon it became impossible to book a table for dinner. Almost overnight "Retro" had jump-started a gastronomic renaissance of sorts in the capital city.

Two years later they decided to expand: the box was beginning to feel claustrophobic, no longer able to contain the partners' ambitions. "Ever since the beginning, we've made a point of being linear, taking great Italian ingredients and elevating them, without creating absurd mash-ups of flavors. But at one point, the cuisine we were making felt a little bit too simple," laughs Alessandro. "We felt we were ready to get behind a more powerful engine." As we speak, his eyes dart from place to person, recording every detail, on high alert in case someone from the kitchen rushes in with a query. ("Chef, how can I tell if the sage kombucha is ready?") Giuseppe, the other half of Retro, who over time has given up kitchen duties to oversee front of house operations, is a quieter presence, a true problem solver, ready to anticipate every client's requests and to read Alessandro's mind, surely racking up a few thousand steps each day along the corridor that connects front and back of house.

The new Retrobottega is a sleek cocoon: straight lines, no handles, nothing protruding; wood (the expensive kind), slate and steel countertops and tables, cement floors, resin walls, an antique ceiling, hanging low. Rough and polished, just like its cuisine. Because the building is old, the firm in charge of renovations faced considerable architectural constraints. "Initially we wanted to have just one extra-long counter, spanning the whole length of the space, where all customers would eat facing the cooks at work. It proved to be structurally impossible, so we kept the idea of a main longitudinal axis, with an open view kitchen running front to back, two communal tables, a six-seat counter, and a corridor which is like the spinal cord of the restaurant." It was a functional choice: the work flow of each kitchen station is optimized this way, and the front of house can always keep an eye on both tables and dishes as they are being prepared.

Miocchi's dishes have an almost tangible, sometimes brutal physicality, where an obsession with textures is barely tamed by a few classical touches. They are as flavorful as they are aestheticized—the way they're composed and plated, the way each surface in the restaurant serves as a theatrical backdrop for the food. Alessandro's thought process often starts with the memory of a flavor, like that of the *melanzana al funghetto* (which, despite the name, has no mushrooms in it, and is usually made of just eggplant and tomato) his dad used to make for him.

"We are recipients of Italian flavors passed down from generation to generation; we absorb them. I'm equally at ease with lamb, pigeon, or duck because they're part of my culinary roots, because I remember them. My job is to make them contemporary, through technique. Which is the reason why, for instance, I pretreat all of the poultry with a honey and salt brine: I do it because I don't really trust anybody to salt the meat the way I want, but mainly because it relaxes the fibers and it allows me to use even the toughest parts of the animal." While meat (mostly offal and less noble cuts) is certainly well represented on Retrobottega's menu, foraged vegetables are at its core.

Foraging is Alessandro's specialty. It's his passion, driven by study and by a quasi-religious admiration for Noris Cunaccia, the magnetic "lady of foraging" who every season beckons hordes of enthusiasts to the

fields and forests of her beloved Dolomites. ("She's a goddess.") Alessandro forages every week. Depending on the season and the weather he'll go to either Lazio or to Abruzzo, mainly on the Maiella massif.

"We pick what is there. Nothing is predetermined, there's very little we can control: what we see is what we get."

He can't go out with the idea for a dish and find something that fits: it's the other way around. "We pick linden flowers, nettle, dandelion greens, pine needles. What we were thinking in the beginning was, should we make a risotto with them? Should we puree them? It was limiting. We knew these herbs and vegetables had to be central, not peripheral."

One day, as he was consulting his French cookbooks (France is an important reference for Miocchi, a consequence of working under Crippa and Genovese) he came across the recipe for a liver crepinette, a classic sausage-like preparation, wrapped in caul fat. "I had all those leftover stalks, from cleaning the foraged greens. My staff would wait for me to be gone to throw them out: they wanted to make room in the walk-ins but I'd get so mad! So one day I decided to use them for a version of crepinette. It's the only dish that's been on the menu for three years straight: we use different vegetables depending on the season, but it's always there. Dressed with a French sauce."

Over time, Miocchi has created a geo-temporal map of his foraging, charting everything he picks against location and calendar, creating endless lists of species and varieties, tubers, roots, buds, leaves, flowers. He ferments, preserves, makes syrups. In an elusive science such as foraging, it all makes for a more organized approach, allowing him to plan ahead and experiment. "For instance, I used last year's pinecone syrup to dress this year's Vacca Vecchia steak with string beans; and I paired sea snails with silver fir shoots, which to me taste a bit like garlic and a bit like clams: I used them with snail-shaped pasta, lumache. The shape of the pasta—almost like a shell—traps the snails inside, making for the perfect bite." The lumache are made at Retrobottega Pasta, the restaurant's own fresh pasta lab, right next door (there is also an enoteca, with a curated selection of wines and Retro-style snacks). "The pasta lab has allowed us to do things like the leaf lasagna, where we take paper-thin layers of green pasta, made with seaweed, and fill them with wild leaves and cheese. I enjoy playing with shapes; it satisfies my need for visual stimulation."

Retrobottega is open all day, every day, except for Mondays. These extended hours may be the norm elsewhere, but not so in Italy, where restaurants serve food at given hours: lunch and dinner, nothing before, after, or in between (bars and *tavole calde*, the Italian equivalent of a diner, are in a category of their own and operate nonstop).

It's a lot of work for Retrobottega's team. "But eventually we all rest. When I'm off, I like to eat spaghetti al pomodoro. It resets the palate. It's soothing; it says 'chill out, you're not on duty today.'"

Brioche al Polline e Gelato di Fiori
Bee Pollen Glazed "Maritozzo" with Wildflower Gelato

This brioche bun is inspired by the sweet Roman roll, *maritozzo*, which is normally filled with whipped cream. Retrobottega uses honey from the local sulla flower, but you can substitute any mild, light-colored honey to make your ice cream. Locust bean gum (LBG), also known as carob bean gum, is a white powder made from the seeds of the carob tree and serves as a natural thickener. It's not to be confused with the brown carob powder that is often used as a chocolate substitute.

Brioche Buns
4 cups (1 lb. 2 oz.) unbleached bread flour
2/3 cup sugar
2 teaspoons salt
Finely grated zest of 1 lemon
½ cup creamy levain (see page 39)
1 ½ teaspoons active dry yeast
6 medium eggs
½ cup plus 1 tablespoon unsalted butter cut into pieces, room temperature

Bee Pollen Syrup
½ cup sugar
½ cup water
3 tablespoons bee pollen

To finish
Wildflower gelato (recipe follows)
Edible flowers such as acacia, elderflower, dandelion, or chamomile, for garnish

Makes 8 brioche rolls

For the brioche buns
In the bowl of a stand mixer fitted with a dough hook, stir together flour, sugar, salt, and lemon zest. Add levain, yeast, and eggs. Mix on low speed until gluten has developed and dough passes "the window pane test," (taking a small portion of dough and stretching it gently between your thumbs and first two fingers until it resembles a translucent membrane: if it doesn't break, it's ready) 5 to 10 minutes. Increase speed to medium-low and gradually add the butter, 1 tablespoon at a time, working the dough for 1 minute in between each addition. When the dough is shiny, smooth, and all the butter has been incorporated, scrape out onto a well-floured surface.

Fold dough in fourths, flip it over, then turn and pull with your hands until you form a ball. Transfer to a large, clean bowl, cover tightly with plastic wrap and place in the refrigerator overnight.

The next day, remove the dough from the refrigerator and bring to room temperature, about 1 hour. Scrape onto a clean, lightly floured work surface and cut into 8 portions with a dough scraper or knife. With floured hands, shape into balls and place on lightly greased or parchment-lined baking sheet, leaving 2 to 3 inches between each ball. Cover the balls with a clean cloth, and let them rise until they've doubled in size (this may take as little as 45 minutes; or up to 2 hours, depending on the warmth of the room).

For the bee pollen syrup
In a small saucepan over medium heat, combine water and sugar and cook, stirring occasionally until sugar dissolves completely, about 5 minutes. Remove from heat and set aside to cool. When the syrup has cooled completely, stir in the bee pollen.

To finish
Preheat oven to 325°F, fill a loaf pan with a couple of inches of water and place on the bottom of the oven to create steam. Cook until buns are golden, 14 to 16 minutes. Remove from oven and brush immediately with bee pollen syrup. Set aside to cool completely.

When ready to serve, split buns open with a sharp knife and fill with wildflower gelato. Garnish with fresh flowers and serve immediately.

Wildflower Gelato
1 cup fresh, edible flowers such as acacia, elderflower, dandelion, or chamomile
2 cups whole milk
1 cup whipping cream
½ cup mild, pale honey
¼ teaspoon locust bean gum

Wash and spin-dry the flowers. Place them in an airtight container with the milk, close tightly and chill in the refrigerator for 48 hours. Pour the milk through a fine mesh sieve into a medium bowl; discard the flowers.

Combine the cream and honey in a small saucepan over low heat and stir until honey has dissolved completely into the cream. Remove from heat, let cool slightly, whisk in the locust bean gum, and set aside to cool completely.

Pour the cooled cream-honey mixture into the infused milk, and stir to combine. Cover tightly with plastic wrap and chill in refrigerator for at least 2 hours, preferably overnight.

Pour the chilled mixture into an ice cream maker and follow the manufacturer's instructions. Transfer the churned ice cream to an airtight container and freeze until ready to use.

Pasta in Bianco, Mandorle e Aglio
Pasta with Green Almonds and Garlic

Green almonds have an infuriatingly fleeting moment, before they harden into the brown almonds we're familiar with. If you're lucky enough to live near an almond-producing region, you will be able to find these delicate nuts between mid-April and mid-June.

16 oz. unpeeled green almonds
¼ cup whole, raw almonds
4 cloves of garlic, peeled, plus ¼ clove
¾ cup extra-virgin olive oil
2 tablespoons plus ¾ teaspoon salt, divided
½ teaspoon ground black pepper, or more to taste
12 oz. spaghetti or fettuccini
2 tablespoons finely grated raw almonds, for garnish
20 wild garlic or chive flowers, for garnish

Serves 4

Clean the green almonds: slice through the hull with a paring knife and split open to reveal the soft nut inside. Remove the nut to a medium-sized bowl and set aside the hull. Repeat with remaining green almonds, reserve hulls.

Thinly slice 2 cloves of garlic and place in a small bowl. Cover with cold water and chill in refrigerator overnight.

The next day, preheat oven to 350° F. Spread the whole, raw almonds on a baking sheet and toast in the oven, stirring occasionally, until golden and fragrant, 7 to 10 minutes. Remove from oven and transfer to a small bowl while hot. Cover with ½ cup cold water and soak at room temperature for 3 hours. Strain the almonds and reserve the soaking water.

In a blender, combine green almonds, toasted almonds, ¼ clove of garlic, ½ cup reserved soaking water, ¼ cup extra-virgin olive oil, ¾ teaspoon salt, and ½ teaspoon pepper; blend until smooth. The mixture should be the consistency of thick pesto. Taste for salt and add more if desired.

To make the broth, combine green almond hulls, 2 cloves of garlic and 1 quart of water in a medium saucepan over medium-high heat. Bring to a boil, immediately remove from heat and cover. Let stand at room temperature for about 1 hour. Filter the almond broth through a fine mesh strainer into a bowl; set aside.

Heat ½ cup extra-virgin olive oil in a small skillet over medium-high heat. Drain the garlic slices and pat dry with paper towels. When the oil is hot and shimmering but not smoking, add the garlic slices and fry, stirring occasionally, until light golden and fragrant, about 1 minute.

Fill a large pot with water and bring to a boil over high heat. Add 2 tablespoons of salt. Boil the pasta for half of the time indicated on the package, then drain. Transfer half-cooked pasta to a large saucepan over medium heat, add 1 cup of almond broth and continue to cook, stirring occasionally until pasta is al dente, adding more broth if necessary, until pasta is shiny and the broth has evaporated. Remove from heat and stir in the almond pesto.

Divide pasta between 4 warm plates, and top with grated almonds, fried garlic, and wild garlic or chive flowers.

FRANCESCO & VINCENZO

MONTARULI

When brothers Francesco and Vincenzo Montaruli were little, their father, a farmer, would take them out to the Altopiano delle Murge. This karst plateau, barren and moon-like between the Tavoliere delle Puglie ("Italy's barn," sown with wheat and oat), to the north, and picture-perfect Salento, to the south, is where he'd go to pick wild vegetables. They didn't call it "foraging" back then; it was known as *andar per campi* (walking the fields). It was a necessity. "One day, many years later," recalls Vincenzo, "as we were leaving for a food conference, with a bag full of asphodels, my dad told us, 'It must be nice to go to Milan and play artists for a day with your wildflowers. We used to eat those for breakfast; they'd keep us going while working in the fields.'"

Something else he recalls from those early days on the Murge was a man with a majestic mustache zooming by on a 1972 Gilera motorcycle with off-road wheels. He never wore a helmet, and strapped behind his seat were bundles of weeds and flowers so big they covered his license plate. That man is Francesco Gargano or, as everyone calls him, "Ciccillo." One day he showed up at the Montaruli's restaurant, offering to sell a bunch of wild asparagus. Since then, they've been inseparable.

It's late, and we're having a glass of wine at Mezza Pagnotta, the Montarulis' fifteen-seat restaurant in the center of Ruvo di Puglia, a small town not far from Bari, in the upper half of the "boot's" heel. There's a narrow entrance, a tall reclaimed-wood counter topped with jugs full of carob seeds and legumes, white stone walls covered in tapestries of dried wild herbs, tomatoes, and peppers, and limestone floors that reflect the warm, soft glow of the restaurant's lights, which are encased in hand-carved pieces of hardwood. Round, bright red Ethiopian eggplants and okra pods spill out of wicker baskets by the door. It's midweek and the restaurant is full. A woman at the table next to ours asks for a menu. Francesco smiles. Mezza Pagnotta serves only a handful of dishes, cooked in an oven or on a small induction plate, in a stamp-sized kitchen. Francesco, who is in charge of service, also acts as a walking menu, as there isn't a written one.

Ninety-five percent of dishes here are plant-based. The only animal proteins served come from eggs and goat cheese, and even those are used sparingly. There is no pasta, even though this is orecchiette land, because they feel it would take away from the true hero of their cuisine: greens. There is bread, however, baked by Vincenzo using only old varieties of local durum wheat and replacing water with a wild fennel extraction. "There is no burrata or *cicoria e favetta*, either," says Francesco proudly, referring to the two staples (burrata cheese and chicory with fava beans) of most local restaurants, particularly those catering to tourists.

Of the vegetables that comprise each day's offering, a good two-thirds are provided by Ciccillo and grow freely on the Murge. As Vincenzo stays behind to man the kitchen and tend to the restaurant's small vegetable plot, Francesco picks in the wild with Ciccillo. "I still think he's a rock star, even though now I know he's actually considered an outcast, someone who lives on the fringes of society. He turned his back on agriculture, the main source of income around here, and relied on what he can harvest from nature for sustenance. The Murge are such an inherent part of his life he starts developing hives if he misses a day out."

Francesco has a diploma in accounting, but since he and Vincenzo (who dropped out of school at twelve to work in restaurants) opened their first business, a street food joint, he started educating himself in botany; he's been studying Ciccillo and others like him, trying to school himself on the properties of local plants and their cultural and historical significance. The Montarulis were already serving flavors of the Murge between two slices of bread at their street food joint, but at Mezza Pagnotta they took it up a notch. They describe their cuisine as *cucina etnobotanica*. "Puglia's biodiversity is incredible and yet the boys and girls of Ruvo di Puglia wouldn't be able to tell fennel fronds from dill. People used to select, cook, and eat ingredients for flavor as well as for their beneficial properties. They'd pick wild cardoon around Easter because their cooking water could detox the liver after the holiday's big meals. They'd dig up lampascioni, or hyacinth bulbs, for their invigorating effects: they're like natural bitters. We sometimes serve them before meals to stimulate the appetite."

The brothers feel closer to northern Africa and the Middle East than to Denmark: the kinship stems from sharing what they call a *sentimento mediterraneo*. So many of the ingredients used are the same, so many of the preparations similar. "In front of hummus or baba ganoush we're all equal," says Francesco, who has traveled with Vincenzo to cook in Lebanon, Egypt, and Tunisia, and whose favorite cookbook author is unsurprisingly Yotam Ottolenghi. This Mediterranean sentiment is at the core of the restaurant's philosophy, together with a reverence for a certain primal instinct, one that is dormant in so many of us. "It's the instinct that allows us to fend for ourselves in nature and it's our duty to awaken it, if we want to feel truly alive."

Which is what we set out to do the next morning: When we meet back at the restaurant, Alberto and I are sleepy, groggy, slow. Not exactly primal instinct material. Francesco greets us with a steaming cup of "shepherd's tea." "Drink this up," he commands. "It'll revive you." It's made with Clinopodium suaveolens (a short plant with purple flowers locals call "acino pugliese"), and it's known to lower the body temperature, a natural antipyretic. Already feeling better, we drive out to the plateau.

Ciccillo is with us: he's short, stocky, his mustache almost all white though still majestic. He doesn't speak much, occasionally giving Francesco directions in the local dialect, and as we drive his eyes dart back and forth, scanning the land. I can tell he's eager to get out of the car, and as soon as we stop, he bolts. I am reminded of what Francesco had told me the day before: "Ciccillo is in his mid-seventies but he has the strength of a twenty-year-old."

I spend the following hours in a trance. We pick wild cardoons, which grow close to the ground, to absorb heat during the cold winter months. They're like "vegetable octopuses": shaped much like them, they retract their leaves as if they were tentacles when immersed in cold water. Francesco and Ciccillo expertly extract them and then rub their calloused fingers along the leaves to remove the thorns. Ciccillo shows me the milk oozing from the cut roots, which can be used as a clotting agent, like rennet. The most tender of the roots are candied, the toughest are replanted.

Francesco points at a gariga, a round-shaped cluster of herbs, typical of this area: this particular formation, a huddle of plants, traps humidity and protects the shrub from the winds and the sun. We see wild radishes and a meadow saffron flower, dangerously similar to the real deal, but toxic. There are giant fennel bushes (Ferula communis), also toxic but useful: with the bamboo-like stalks the locals build lightweight pieces of furniture, while the mushrooms that grow on the plant are considered a delicacy. More delicious mushrooms, of the king trumpet kind, can be found near the field eryngo, also known for its use in herbal medicine.

Francesco explains that many of the plants that go well together in a dish also grow next to each other in the fields: nature acts as a flavor match-maker.

So much knowledge, so little time to absorb it all. For this purpose, the Montarulis have launched the "Stai brado" (Stay wild) project, a series of immersive workshops that start on the Murge and end up in the kitchen: a way to reconnect their clients to what their land has to offer. It's a reconnection many restaurateurs of the area seem to be longing for, as they ask Francesco to supply them with wild cardoons and other products of the Murge. He's happy to do it.

Back at the restaurant, it's time to eat. With no clear division between appetizers and entrees, we feast on vegetable dishes that feel as warm, satisfying, and flavorful as any lasagna. We finish with a baked pear, of the Coscia variety (page 109), glazed with carob chocolate and served with a wild mint-infused fresh cream and a mother tincture of acino pugliese. In my experience of the new cucina italiana, desserts have proven to be the one thing that needs improving, still. They tend to be either too French or too conceptual and minimalistic, lacking a true identity. But a baked pear, simple, clean, and still delicious: I can't think of a more Italian dessert than this.

Pera Coscia al Cioccolato di Carrube e Crema al Latte con Menta Selvatica

Poached Pears in Carob Chocolate with Minted Milk Cream

The Montaruli brothers make their carob molasses (which they call "chocolate") out of actual dried carob pods, but we replaced them with carob powder for your convenience. When making the Minted Milk Cream, use wild mint if available.

Pears
4 small pears, washed
4 ½ cups water
1 cup sugar
Minted milk sauce, for serving (recipe follows)

Carob Sauce
2/3 cup water
¼ cup sugar
1 cup carob powder
¼ cup heavy cream

For the pears
Cut a thin slice off the bottom of each pear so it can stand up on its own; do not peel pears. Combine water and sugar in a medium saucepan over medium-high heat and stir to combine. When sugar has dissolved and mixture begins to boil, gently lower the pears into saucepan, turning occasionally to make sure they are completely covered by the liquid. If they aren't submerged, transfer to a smaller pan. Cook at a gentle simmer for 10 minutes, remove from heat, and let pears cool completely in the syrup. When cool, gently transfer pears to a rack to dry.

For the carob sauce
Combine water and sugar in a small saucepan over medium heat. Stir occasionally until sugar dissolves and mixture begins to simmer. Lower heat to the minimum and slowly sift in the carob powder, a little at a time, whisking energetically until well combined. Cook for 5 minutes, whisking constantly, until the mixture is steaming, shiny, and thick. Very slowly stir in the heavy cream, a little at a time, whisking until shiny. Remove from heat. Set aside to cool slightly.

Carefully spoon the carob sauce over the pears on the cooling rack, making sure to completely coat the pears (place a plate or parchment paper underneath the grate to collect drips). Transfer pears to the refrigerator until ready to serve, for about an hour, or until carob coating appears glossy.

Spoon a generous helping of minted milk cream in the center of each of four plates and place a pear on top. Serve immediately.

Minted milk cream
2 cups whole milk
1 cup loosely packed mint leaves
¼ cup sugar
¼ cup potato starch

Combine milk and mint leaves in a small saucepan over medium heat. Bring to a boil and then remove immediately from heat. Cover with lid and set aside to cool for 30 minutes at room temperature. Transfer to refrigerator and chill for 6 to 12 hours.

Filter milk through a fine mesh sieve set over a saucepan, pressing and squeezing mint leaves to release all the liquid. Discard leaves. Add sugar and stir over low heat until dissolved. When mixture is hot and steaming, but not yet simmering, whisk in potato starch and cook, mixing constantly, until mixture has thickened, 7 to 10 minutes. Remove from heat and set aside to cool at room temperature. Refrigerate until ready to serve, up to 2 days.

GIANLUCA GORINI
BENEDETTO RULLO
LORENZO STEFANINI
STEFANO TONGI
RICCARDO GIRAUDI

SUNDAY RESTAURAT-EURS

GIANLUCA

GORINI

"I usually pick a few cherries straight from the tree late in the morning, when it's just about getting warm. They're so sweet it's like eating a piece of pastry, the best breakfast ever! It's atomico!"

Gianluca Gorini says "atomico" a lot: it reflects his indefatigable optimism. Originally from Pesaro, a seaside town in le Marche, a region on the Adriatic Sea wedged between Emilia-Romagna, Umbria, and Abruzzo, thanks to his buoyant personality he could very well pass for someone who was born and raised in exuberant Romagna. One of his favorite catch phrases is "L'ottimismo è il profumo della vita" (optimism is the scent of life), the slogan of a famous commercial from the early 2000s.

Gorini ("Gian" for his friends) is like a jockey (slender, compact), with beautiful hazel eyes ("The longest eyelashes I've ever seen on a man!" says our photographer) and a child-like smile; when not in chef's whites he often wears jeans, a polo shirt, and carries a messenger bag. He doesn't look a day older than twenty-eight (he's in his mid-thirties). But as soon as one gets to know him a little better, two things become evident: first, he's a natural born prankster, and second, he's one of Italy's most talented chefs, with an almost militaristic focus when in service.

We're meeting him at Azienda Agricola Piera Casadei near Cesena, in the heart of Romagna (a district known for the outstanding quality of its produce), where he gets most of the vegetables and fruit for DaGorini, the Michelin-starred restaurant he runs with his wife Sara. Twenty-four varieties of cherries are grown here, as well as apricots, artichokes, snow peas, asparagus, tomatoes, and several kinds of cabbages. Impossibly tall bamboo plants are kept for their shoots, which are lychee-like in texture and taste like artichoke. There are patches of wild strawberries that originated from one tiny plant and spread like wildfire; the son of the owner hands me one: it tastes like a zinfandel grape. The family—mother, father, two sons—pick everything by hand, with no hired help. There are seven hectares of land to maintain. Interestingly, it will take a bit of arm-twisting to get the Casadeis to agree to let me print their name. In a world of fame-seekers, they're quite the opposite: one of the reasons Gorini likes them so much. The other reason has to with a sense of place, which is at the heart of his culinary philosophy.

"I think of my cuisine as my attempt to represent the profound nature of what we have here, filtered through my own nature," says Gian. This comes with an awareness of the place, of what it has to offer. It's not about being "regional," it's being "local" and "personal." Depending on what your personality tells you, "local" can mean your village, your region, or Italy itself. "It's subjective, and that is the beauty of it," he explains. "But it has to be authentic, and it doesn't have to feel restraining." He continues: "There are countless chefs with sound technique, in some cases better than mine. So how do I get people to come back to my restaurant, which is a very simple restaurant, not a luxurious one? How do I get them to come back, maybe driving for a hundred kilometers on a school night? The answer is authenticity, truth. If you eat my lamb and you say 'wow,' well, I can show you where that wow comes from."

The lamb thigh, served with a pesto of sundried tomatoes, dandelion, anchovies, garlic, and licorice (recipe on page 123) and dressed with a garlic sauce, is indeed wow-worthy, as is the pigeon (a Gorini signature dish), served with a bay leaf extraction, its giblets skewered and presented separately. Both meats, as are almost all meats at DaGorini's, are cooked on a very small round grill, something one wouldn't expect to find used so extensively in a Michelin-starred restaurant.

The big misconception about grilling is that it's primal, therefore not technical. Far from it: it's as technical as it gets. One has to know how to "read" a piece of meat, at sight and by touch, in order to let each cut best express itself. It's a very difficult cooking style to teach (Gorini hosts stagiaires in his kitchen "and they all prefer to cook meat sous-vide: you bag it up, you set the temperature, you let it go..."), but he loves his way because it says something about his chops: it shows he's serious about them; it presents the ingredient almost unadorned.

Gorini sources his goats and sheep from a local farm. In between services he takes us to see it, and we watch the herd of immaculate Saanen, Chamois Coloured (an Alpine goat, brown with a black stripe along its back), and black and white Maltese hop over a small stream, back from pasture. As idyllic as it seems, we know this is a difficult life. "I buy the whole animal and go pick it up at the slaughterhouse, not the most time-efficient thing for me. This is why many restaurateurs prefer to buy already portioned lambs from abroad and why breeders struggle to make ends meet," says Gianluca. Each animal produces two liters of milk a day, on average. They give birth only once a year. Do the math: it's hard to make it this way. The most reliable source of income for the farmers is the sale of goat's milk to the San Patrignano rehab community.

Gorini told them it would be more efficient if they sold older goats, weighing about thirty kilos (the meat waste after processing would be less, and the flavor more interesting). But their habits are hard to change, so Gianluca is not sure they'll follow his advice.

Back at the restaurant, Sara Gorini has just finished up the simple mise en place. A quick peek in the kitchen and we get to say hi to her mother, who helps keep things clean and tidy when service is particularly busy. We taste a superb dish: it's fresh pasta bottoni (round, dome-like "buttons"), filled with fava bean puree and sheep's milk cheese and served in a sheep's broth. This dish is emblematic of Gorini's cuisine: rustic yet technical, with a certain straight, no-bullshit elegance. It's an ode to a place, this place. It's local, which doesn't mean traditional: everything about Gorini's cuisine is contemporary. "Tradition comes from the recipes; regionality—or locality—comes from the products. Foreigners still see us as the country of tradition and great ingredients, and we have a duty to move forward, building upon this."

Take Gorini's Passatelli in Brodo (recipe on page 121). Historically this is a farmers' dish from Romagna: rugged cylinders of pasta made with breadcrumbs, Parmesan cheese, egg and nutmeg, served in a meat broth.

Gorini serves his in a broth made with all the scraps left from prepping cabbages during the winter, a liquid so rich in color and flavor it tastes almost like diluted soy sauce. It's briny, with a slight, almost undetectable, pleasant bitterness–just like the bottoni with fava bean puree.

To those who don't know him well, Gorini is in fact known as "the king of bitterness." It goes back to his days at Ristorante Le Giare, in Montiano (about an hour from DaGorini). Prior to that, he had served for four years

under his mentor, Paolo Lopriore (see page 44); many (including Gianluca) refer to him as a "misunderstood genius." One of Lopriore's trademarks, especially back in the days of Il Canto, in Siena (where he first gained then scandalously lost one Michelin star), was a tendency to favor a sometimes aggressively bitter flavor profile. Gorini had seemingly inherited that trait, at least in the first years of his career. "I am and forever will be known as 'Lopriore's protégé' and there's no escaping this label."

It's a difficult legacy to carry and even though he will always be grateful to his master for opening an impressive culinary horizon to him, he is now his own person. Even his "signature bitterness" is much tamer than it used to be. "It reflects my growth as a man. When I was at Le Giare, I wanted to show off, I felt like I had something to prove. But it was almost an academic exercise for me. I wanted people to say 'fuck, that's extreme!' I had forgotten that the first commandment of a chef is to make good dishes. I mean, look, all excesses are detrimental in the end."

At DaGorini's, Gian is more calm, more resolute. And that translates into his dishes, the choices he makes in the kitchen. He finally remembered why he got into this brutal, crazy fifteen-hour-straight-workdays business in the first place: he loves to cook. Gorini grew up in a family trattoria and that is the style of hospitality he likes. "It's what we Italians are really known for, yet we've never been able to maximize its value: for thirty years we've been too busy looking at what Spain, France, then Scandinavia were doing. I owe it to Adrià if I can mix the tradition of a trattoria with my own rigor and technical background, but the real turning point for

me was adding my personal touch, a certain sentiment. If my young son today is free to walk between the tables barefoot during service, then I feel I've done something right."

It's time to leave, as Gorini has to prep before leaving for Spessore. This particular event is part of a circuit of food festivals (including Borderwine, Scamporella, Fuoco, and Almeni) that are redefining the way the young guns of Italian cuisine come together. They are collaborative bacchanals held in the provinces of Italy and open to the public where Michelin-star chefs cook alongside fry cooks and pit-masters. They are built around the concept of conviviality and are a collective experimentation on comfort, often with the common denominator of natural wine or artisanal beer.

"One of the distinctive traits of this 'new cucina italiana' movement is precisely this collaborative spirit, something relatively unheard of in our industry up until a few years ago. The reason, I believe, is that we now have distinctive, well-formed ideas and personalities, so there's no fear of mixing them up with those of others. Don't get me wrong: not all my young colleagues are doing things I like—sometimes I'll see a dish and wonder, 'what the hell was he thinking?' But overall, I see a great team shaping up. And we're all friends and we all really like to have fun. What more could you want?!"

Passatelli Romagnoli, Brodo di Verza, Semi di Zucca e Soia

Passatelli, Savoy Cabbage Broth, Pumpkin Seeds, and Soy Sauce

According to experts, this pasta, made with breadcrumbs, grated Parmigiano, eggs, and very little flour, was first born in Romagna and then became popular in Emilia. Gianluca Gorini serves his in a broth made with the tough, external leaves of the Savoy cabbage, to reduce waste in his kitchen. Traditionally passatelli are extruded (from which they get their name: "passare" means "to go through") with a special press, but you can use a potato ricer with large holes.

Broth

2/3 cup fresh, raw pumpkin seeds
6-7 leaves of Savoy cabbage, tough external leaves preferred
¼ cup soy sauce

Passatelli

2 cups lightly-packed, finely grated Parmigiano Reggiano
1 cup plus 1 tablespoon unsalted dried breadcrumbs
scant ½ cup all-purpose flour
3 eggs
1 egg white
1/8 teaspoon salt
1/8 teaspoon freshly grated nutmeg
½ teaspoon freshly grated lemon zest

Special equipment:
Sturdy, large-holed potato ricer, or passatelli press

Serves 4-6

Preheat oven to 350°F. Spread the pumpkin seeds in a single layer on a baking sheet and bake for 1 hour or until the seeds are dark golden brown with black spots on them.

Place a large, nonstick frying pan over medium-high heat. When the pan is hot, add a couple of cabbage leaves to the dry pan and toast until golden, 2 to 3 minutes per side. Repeat with remaining cabbage leaves.

Combine toasted pumpkin seeds and cabbage leaves in a medium stockpot. Add 6 cups of water, bring to a boil over high heat, and then simmer over very low heat for 45 to 60 minutes. Remove from heat and let cool at room temperature.

Meanwhile, bring soy sauce to a boil in a small saucepan over medium-high heat, then lower to a simmer and cook until it has reduced by 80%, about 10 minutes. Filter reduced soy sauce and the cabbage broth with a fine mesh strainer. Combine the two liquids in an airtight container; you should have about 3 to 3 ½ cups total liquid. Cover and refrigerate overnight.

The next day, combine all passatelli ingredients in a large bowl and mix with a wooden spoon until a shaggy dough forms. Turn out onto a clean surface and knead briefly by hand to form a smooth dough, 3 to 4 minutes. Wrap in a clean, damp kitchen towel and set aside to rest for at least 1 hour.

Remove broth from the refrigerator and warm in a medium-sized saucepan over medium-low heat, but do not boil.

Bring a large pot of water to a boil over high heat; add 2 tablespoons of salt. Place a handful the passatelli dough into a large-holed potato ricer. Working over the pot of boiling water, press the dough through the ricer, and scrape off the strands with a sharp knife, allowing the strands to fall directly into the boiling water. Strands should be about the length of your index finger. Cook until the strands float to the top, about 1 minute. Remove the passatelli from water with a spider strainer or a large slotted spoon, and transfer them to serving bowls. Add a ladleful (about ½ cup) of warm broth to the bowl and serve hot. Repeat with remaining dough and broth.

Agnello alla Brace, Pesto Nero, Aglio Dolce e Cicoria
Grilled Lamb with Black Pesto, Sweet Garlic, and Chicory

So much of what shapes the cuisines of young Italian chefs has to do with a sort of "flavor canon," a series of ideal pairings one absorbs viscerally, mainly through the experience of domestic food—flavor coding is the real lesson of the nonne. Gianluca Gorini is no exception: This dish is all about the aromatics of the black pesto, garlic, and sundried tomatoes. Gorini chooses a non-traditional rub for lamb, because it reminds him of when he'd wake up on Sundays to the almost-burnt smell of verdure gratinate.

Black pesto
1 1/3 cup loosely packed flat-leaved parsley leaves
1 cup loosely packed fresh basil leaves
¾ cup wild fennel fronds
3 tablespoons fresh marjoram leaves
3 tablespoons fresh thyme leaves
1 salt-packed anchovy, rinsed
½ clove garlic, peeled
3 tablespoons oil-packed taggiasche or other small, black olives
½ cup extra-virgin olive oil

Lamb
1 head of garlic, plus 1 clove of unpeeled garlic
2 cups goat's milk, divided
1 rack of lamb (about 2 lbs.), at room temperature
2 tablespoons extra-virgin olive oil
Salt
1 head of Catalogna chicory, or other chicory
4 sundried tomatoes, soaked and chopped

Serves 4

Combine all the ingredients for the black pesto in a small saucepan over very low heat. Cook until herbs are crisp and toasted, but not burnt, 25 to 30 minutes. Remove from heat and strain the mixture with a fine mesh strainer; reserving the cooking oil. Transfer the cooked herbs and solids to a small mixer fitted with a metal blade and blend until finely chopped. While the machine is running on low, slowly add the reserved cooking oil until you have a dense, pesto-like sauce. Set aside.

Peel the garlic cloves, slice in half lengthwise and remove the green germ from the inside. Place the garlic in a small saucepan and cover with 1/3 cup of goat's milk; bring to a boil over medium heat. Cook for 2 minutes then strain garlic; discard milk. Return the garlic to the saucepan and repeat this process 4 more times; bring to a boil with 1/3 cup of fresh goat's milk each time, drain, and repeat. Transfer the garlic to a small mixer or blender, and blend with remaining goat's milk until smooth. Add salt to taste and set aside.

Rub the rack of lamb with 1 tablespoon of extra virgin olive oil, and salt generously. Prepare your barbecue and light briquettes with a chimney starter. Preheat oven to 120°F, or the lowest heat setting. When the coals are ready, place the rack of lamb on the grill over the coals. Cook, turning occasionally, until well browned but still rare inside, 7 to 8 minutes. Remove from heat and transfer to a rimmed baking sheet. Place in warm oven to rest for 25 to 30 minutes. If your oven is hotter than 120°F, turn it off as soon as you put the lamb in the oven.

Meanwhile, prepare the chicory: wash the leaves and cut away the hard center rib; pat leaves dry with paper towels. Heat a tablespoon of olive oil in a large skillet over medium-high heat. When the oil is hot, add a whole, unpeeled garlic clove and the chicory leaves. Sauté briefly until the chicory is just wilted, about 1 minute. Remove garlic clove and salt to taste.

Cut the lamb between bones and divide among 4 plates. Drizzle with garlic sauce and garnish with black pesto. Add a few leaves of sautéed chicory and chopped sundried tomatoes to each plate. Serve immediately.

BENEDETTO RULLO, LORENZO STEFANINI, & STEFANO TERIGI

The guys know how to party. I have seen them in action often enough to know they're fun and they can hold their liquor—whether it's several bottles of the fine natural wine they stock in their cellar, or classic cocktails. I personally witnessed Stefano Terigi—one of the three musketeers who run the kitchen at Ristorante Giglio— ask a friend if he wanted to go grab a Negroni while still holding a gin and tonic in his hand. On more than one occasion we have talked enthusiastically until three in the morning, with no other sound but the soft trickle of water from the fountain on Piazza Antelminelli, where one of their favorite bars is located. One can only imagine how they celebrated upon receiving their first Michelin star in December of 2018.

But they're not a bunch of kitchen brutes: no matter how intense the night is, the following morning they invariably report to the restaurant at 9:30 sharp, and not just out of fear of Signora Paola, Lorenzo's mother, who presides over the restaurant and has been known to verbally smack more than one derriere without batting an eye. They are truly disciplined. Lorenzo Stefanini and Benedetto Rullo are also fathers, and family is their priority: their four kids are regulars at the restaurant, where together with their mothers they usually sit at one of the first tables, under frescoed ceilings, and eat small plates of pasta with butter and Parmesan cheese or thick slices of sourdough bread. Bread is Benedetto's specialty, something all their kids seem to love chomping on, methodically and with eyes half-closed, in a sort of happy, pre-nap trance.

Ristorante Giglio is in Lucca, a Tuscan town hugged by sixteenth-century bastions topped with trees and a panoramic promenade, the birthplace of Giacomo Puccini, not far from the beaches of Versilia. Unlike so much of Tuscany, it evolved beyond the usual lineup of tourist traps, of red and white checkered tablecloths and average pappa al pomodoro (bread and tomato soup, a Tuscan specialty), in favor of restaurants that are gutsy, smart, and deeply satisfying. It has grown to become one of the most vibrant towns in the region.

"This small town has changed so much in the past seventeen years," says Anna Morelli, editor in chief of *Cook_Inc.*, a collectable food publication based out of a salmon-colored villa on the hills outside Lucca, that she runs with her Dutch husband, Frans Vandenberg. Together they have scouted and promoted some of the best culinary talents of the city, including the Giglio guys and Damiano Donati of Fuoco e Materia (see page 82). "Lots of stuff is going on in Lucca in the music, cinema, comics and arts scene in general, and these chefs have contributed to the changes. All of them are in tune with the seasons, all have great respect for ingredients. Each one in its own style has made Lucca a gastronomic destination."

Il Giglio ("Giglio" means lily, an important flower in Tuscan heraldry. Fleur de lys is the symbol of Florence, though here the name comes from the restaurant's location on Piazza del Giglio) was born in 1979 as a spinoff of a historic lucchese restaurant, La Buca di Sant'Antonio. It found its place in town as the quintessential "Sunday restaurant," familiar and poised, serving tradition (like the tordelli, the local ravioli filled with meat, Parmesan, bread, eggs and chard, and topped with ragù) under crystal chandeliers to well-off families and tourists.

"We're bastards when it comes to our culinary style," says Stefano, the Louis Garrel of the trio, the scruffy, ironic one, the one girls swoon over, "because there's three of us and collectively we hail from Calabria, Abruzzo, Lazio, Tuscany, Lombardy, and Venezuela."

Lorenzo and Stefano attended middle school together. Their paths parted for a while, while Stefano studied visual arts in Venice (his dissertation was on Ferran Adrià), and Lorenzo attended Alma, the famous culinary school in Colorno. There he met Benedetto, a Roman kid with a confident, slightly boisterous personality. They all scattered to cut their teeth in different parts of Italy and the world: Lorenzo at La Peca, with chef Antonio Portinari, and at Devero, under Enrico Bartolini, before heading to Tokyo, where he worked at Yppo Isakaya + Aoyagi and at Ryugin; Stefano at Wills Domain, in Australia, at Pierre Gagnaire's Le Solistes in Berlin, and under chef Enrico Crippa, at the three-Michelin-starred restaurant Piazza Duomo, in Alba; Benedetto at Da Vittorio, Le Solistes (where he first met Stefano), and at Christian Puglisi's Relæ, in Copenhagen.

When Lorenzo returned home and started working at Giglio, he thought of calling his friends, rekindling the affinity they had shared. In 2016 they reconvened to run the kitchen, combining not just their regional backgrounds, but also the influences they had absorbed in France, Germany, Denmark, Japan, and Australia. And this, as odd as the thought of a restaurant triumvirate may sound, worked.

Take the Minestra di Triglie, Miso e Shiso (recipe on page 133). Benedetto said he wanted to eat fish soup; the guys got a picture of the day's catch—a gorgeous crate of red mullet—from one of their suppliers, a fisherman in Viareggio. They had the craving, they had the ingredient; short-cut pasta was added to the soup (a very central-southern Italian thing) and finally it was topped with a red mullet tartare, a result of Lorenzo's experience in Japan, something the guys had already tried with a Jack mackerel but didn't really have a place for yet.

"I can't say we have elaborate concepts at the bedrock of our cuisine," says Stefano with a shrug. "We want our dishes to be good, first, and to represent all of us. This restaurant is built around us, as if we were customers: sometimes when we have to come up with a new menu, we sit down and ask each other 'yo, what would you like to eat?'"

Other notable dishes at Giglio include sweetbreads with pumpkin seed paste, pumpkin in saor (a vinegar-based marinade originally used to preserve foods, and common throughout Italy, taking on different names—scapece, carpione—depending on where it is made and what's marinated in it), and grapefruit served with a side of langoustine/bergamot consommé, ravioli filled with sourdough "mayo," spaghetti with pomace and wood pigeon livers; and different renditions of pigeon. "At the moment we grill ours and then marinate it in a liquid made with a very French jus spiked with oil infused with sage, rosemary, thyme, and garlic," explains Lorenzo. "Basically it's roast drippings, but made difficult, because we're a bunch of assholes and we like to make our lives difficult!"

No matter how creative the guys are, there's one traditional dish they know to be untouchable ("If we ever took it off the menu, there'd be a mutiny!"): Pappardelle al Ragu di Frattaglie di Coniglio (Pappardelle with a ragù made of rabbit offal and heads).

The restaurant, after all, is "the fourth chef in the kitchen," with its own personality. Tradition is part of it, and so the troika of human chefs walk a fine line between bourgeoise and hipster, pearls and punk. There are families that still come here decked out for Sunday luncheon (grandmothers with their long strings of pearls, grandchildren fresh from graduation in crisp button-downs) and groups of American tourists, who order the pappardelle, and they easily mix with the cool younger crowd of designers, chefs, and wine producers who come especially for dinner and then hang out with Benedetto, Lorenzo and Stefano until the immaculate linen tablecloths are covered in empty bottles of natural wine, and hip-hop blasts from the speakers in the dining room.

The dining room has also changed—subtly—through the years, with contemporary light fixtures hanging in lieu of the chandeliers and a few sets of Danish and Japanese dishware mixed in with the vintage Ginoris, some flower-encrusted gravy boats almost too pretty for words.

As I write, the guys are preparing to open a new restaurant, Gigliola, a ten-minute walk from Giglio. A fun concept based on deli/rotisserie-to-go, bread, and wine, inspired by the places the guys like to visit when they travel, like Bar Brutal in Barcelona and Tipografia Alimentare in Milan (see page 244). One of the signature dishes of Gigliola will be Pollo Fritto in Salsa Thai. "I loved David Chang's cold fried chicken at Momofuku Ko, in New York," says Benedetto, "and I wanted us to try our hands at it. But there's also the connection with fritto dell'aia, a local fried dish made with chicken and rabbit, bones in, plus sage: it uses a traditional egg-based batter, whereas we use a Japanese 'karaage' batter, something Lorenzo taught us." Only thighs are used, from chickens raised in Garfagnana, a fertile agricultural pocket north of Lucca, also known for its farro, wedged between the Alps and the beginning of the Appenines, and gently dropping towards the sea. It's a crowd-pleaser: Italians love their chicken.

When we met for this book, the guys had just finished drafting a new menu for Giglio: it was inspired by 10 Lezioni di Cucina, Niko Romito's cooking manifesto. (See page 22.) "He is the master," says Lorenzo, who also lists Paolo Lopriore (see page 44), Mauro Uliassi, Enrico Crippa, and Riccardo Camanini (see page 134) among his culinary heroes. "We live in a great time for masterpieces," adds Stefano. Such a good line, I think, as soon as he's finished saying it.

He continues: "There's a tight group of young talents who do their thing, with very personal styles of cooking. For too long we have slacked: we have tourism, so we don't think we have a moral obligation to show what we can really do, and that's so wrong. Whenever I see a lasagna microwaved in a bar it pisses me off. That gives my craft a bad rep, man!"

Minestra di Triglie, Miso e Shiso
Red Mullet, Miso, and Shiso Soup

Stefano Terigi calls this dish "Japan-Viareggio," because it draws from the Tuscan tradition of fish soups, but uses the flavors and techniques from Lorenzo Stefanini's experience in Japan. Note: This recipe calls for a raw red mullet; be aware that it is safest to buy fish that has been previously frozen.

2 lbs. whole red mullet (you may substitute red snapper)
2 tablespoons white miso paste
2 shiso leaves, sliced into thin strips
1 garlic clove, peeled
1 slice of fresh, spicy chile pepper
1 sprig fresh basil
Extra virgin olive oil
½ cup dry white wine
2 fifteen-oz. cans crushed tomatoes
½ teaspoon salt
½ teaspoon sugar
½ cup coarse, homemade breadcrumbs
8 oz. small pasta, like tubetti or ditalini
1 teaspoon finely grated lemon zest

Serves 4

Carefully fillet the red mullet, reserving the heads and bones. Remove skin and pin bones from fillets; cut meat into very small cubes and place in a small bowl. Add miso and shiso; stir to combine. Cover and transfer to refrigerator until ready to serve, up to 2 hours.

Separate basil leaves from stem; set aside leaves and slice the stem into 1-inch segments. Heat 1 tablespoon extra virgin olive oil in a medium saucepan over medium heat. Add garlic clove, chile pepper, and basil stems. Cook, stirring, until fragrant, about 4 minutes. Pour in white wine, and when simmering add crushed tomatoes, salt and sugar; stir and bring to a boil. Lower heat to maintain a steady simmer and cook for 15 minutes. Add fish heads and bones and 1 cup of water; stir to combine. Simmer for 30 minutes, stirring occasionally. Remove from heat and filter through a fine mesh sieve into a small pot. Taste and adjust salt and sugar if necessary to balance the acidity of the tomato. Set aside.

Heat a tablespoon of oil in a nonstick frying pan over medium-high heat. Add breadcrumbs and cook, stirring frequently, until toasted and fragrant, about 7 minutes. Set aside.

Bring a large pot of water to a boil over high heat; add 2 tablespoons of salt. Meanwhile, heat the fish broth over medium-low heat until steaming but not yet simmering. Thinly slice 2 basil leaves. Cook the pasta in the boiling, salted water until al dente. Drain and transfer to a medium bowl; dress with a teaspoon of olive oil, sliced basil and lemon zest.

Divide pasta between 4 bowls, top with a scoop of fish tartare and pour in a generous ladleful of broth. Top with toasted breadcrumbs and serve immediately.

RICCARDO

CAMANINI

I first met Riccardo Camanini at a food festival in Ireland, many years ago. We were talking in our hotel's lobby when I casually said I was a bread baker. I saw his hypnotic, moon-like eyes open, his pupils dilate; he proceeded to grill me with so many questions we sat there until one a.m. Looking at Camanini's intense, ageless face that morning, I remember thinking I had never met a more ambitious person in my life.

Since then, I've felt conflicted about him. I didn't know what to make of his intensity, I was suspicious of his drive. I then came to know him a little better and when I realized how hard he works to live with that drive I recognized something of myself, and suddenly felt closer to him. One of the tools he uses to mitigate that constant inner pull is running. He jogs every morning, along the banks of beautiful lake Garda, where he and his brother Giancarlo manage the one-Michelin-star restaurant Lido 84. When I visited him for this book, I found him with a broken foot and a traction boot, anxious not so much about work, but rather about the forced stop he had had to put on his release valve.

Riccardo Camanini has worked under Gualtiero Marchesi, Raymond Blanc, and Jean-Louis Nomicos, classical training that shaped his technique and imparted a taste for elegance and order. "Elegance" and "order," which you may have heard numerous times in reference to a chef, don't necessarily make for interesting cuisine. But Camanini's is, because it's ambitious yet not perfect.

"When I was little I used to go to a Catholic kindergarten," he remembers, "I hated it there. I lasted three days. One of the most harrowing things about that experience was the school cafeteria, where nuns would

serve us things like re-heated tomato rice." Fragments of that memory, some forty years later, inspired him to create his Riso Riscaldato (recipe on page 141), a dish that to Camanini's own admission, plays with imperfections. "It's different from riso al salto," the crunchy, pan-seared leftover rice: "You can be almost surgical with that, because it's uniformly thin, with an equal proportion of crust and core: the inside stays creamy. With re-heated rice, which you essentially plate by the dollop, the surface is so uneven each bite is different." This imperfection creates peaks of golosità, the elusive quality of something that is delicious beyond logic and interpretation.

Everything about Lido 84—from the garden with its palm trees to the informal efficiency of the front of house, from the handpicked furniture and artworks to the à la carte and tasting menus—speaks of Italy, both eloquently and beautifully. It's powerful because all these elements work together in unison: the Gio Ponti outdoor tables, the conceptual artwork by Stefano Bombardieri, the heavy silver trays stamped with the emblem of the Italian monarchy, a series of gold-rimmed glasses from Ciga Hotels bought at auction, the marble tabletops, the bar with its counter covered in cookbooks, the trolleys, the grand piano, and even the obligatory Ginori plates and Berkel slicer. It's refined and welcoming, the lakeside home you'd expect from a couple of smart, cultivated strivers who have achieved financial success and have started collecting. Which is exactly the case: in the beginning here were banquet tables and cheap tablecloths, no art, and very little money. The Camanini brothers come from a working-class family: they have built Lido from the ground up, buying beauty by the piece, slowly, with hard-earned savings.

And you can feel it. There's a sense of accessibility, which, together with the affordable prices, is probably the reason why the restaurant is always fully booked, often by very young customers. People also love the Camaninis' democratic work policies. The brothers maintain a staff of twenty people, all on regular payroll: they are periodically informed about the restaurant's earnings, and when and if they decide to leave, they can take Riccardo's recipes with them. Then there's the cuisine, a mix of vigorous deliciousness and fodder for brainiacs. Camanini draws from art, anthropology, history, and science. He even requires his staff to do a certain amount of reading every day.

In 2018 he was invited to the Identità Golose's chefs' conference and presented sbernia, a preserved adult sheep, traditionally marinated in wine and herbs and air-dried for weeks by the shepherds of the Val Camonica mountains in Lombardy (his version was covered in honey and beeswax: it looked like an ancient sculpture). At another conference he spoke of how absence fuels creativity, quoting *La leda senza cigno* ("Leda without Swan"), by Gabriele D'Annunzio, whose monumental house museum, Vittoriale, is within walking distance of Lido 84. At the restaurant he serves a dish of fusilli he cooks for a week (alternating cycles of steaming and refrigerating), a process he claims makes the starch in the pasta more digestible. The dish comes with its own explanatory leaflet, and a side of green tomatoes and pistachio sauce.

Interestingly, Camanini's signature dishes are all first courses: spaghettoni with butter and dried yeast (his first hit: a calculated easy win, but still interesting), and Rigatoni Cacio e Pepe in Vescica, which is cooked in a pig's bladder and finished table-side—a very picturesque preparation, which I think is why people like it so much.

Personally, I prefer his green tagliatelle (made with just egg whites and parsley chlorophyll) and agnolotti with white watermelon mustard and hen. I love the beef tartare he serves with pan drippings collected after roasting a whole rabbit and its liver (get some bread, wipe the plate clean), or the Lake Garda sardines, honey-glazed and barbecued the way the locals have traditionally been doing with skewered quails. I believe Camanini is at his best when he's not trying too hard. In a way, he's expressing a similar sentiment when he says, "I don't want to be pigeonholed and I don't like it when people think I'm just a bookworm." And I like when he's cooking what he likes to eat (this is a man who claims he's rather have a hard cookie and a piece of cheese than dessert, and professes his fondness for street food), when he is moved by an ingredient, like the Adriatic bass he waxed poetic about with me for a good five minutes.

There's a little terrace in the back of the restaurant, reserved for the restaurant's staff, where he likes to sit and rest after lunch. The lake's water, just three feet away, makes a lapping sound against the quay. We sit there after lunch, talking about how il Garda permeates everything. It's not just in the products, and not limited to the views and almost blinding light that come in through Lido 84's picture windows. "I think because we're on a lake, no matter how cerebral we get, we can't really ever lose touch with comfort," he says.

Nowhere is this more true than in his desserts. Because Camanini has no pastry training, early on he opted for homemade tarts and cakes. Over the years both restaurant and desserts have become more polished, without losing their coziness. There's Torta di Rose (a staple of northern Italian households, which gets its name from its rose-shaped swirls of flaky, buttery dough) served with zabaglione, and Pan Bagnato, stale bread coated in caramel and served with a blackberry compote and a sumptuous ice cream made with grand cru vanilla from Bora Bora. Camanini says he got the idea for Pan Bagnato from Basque chef Andoni Luis Aduriz, of restaurant Mugaritz, and that he started having his chefs deliver most of dishes to the tables

138

after seeing it done at Noma. He can sometimes be derivative: not a bad thing per se. I like that he credits his sources of inspiration (most of the time). After dessert his chefs present a gigantic string of taffy, pulled as if it was Play-Doh: customers love it.

As the sun starts setting on the mercury-tinged lake surface, Camanini squints. It turns out that he's having problems with his eyesight. I tell him the same has been happening to me. We're getting older. I urge him to get glasses, suggesting his bald, well-shaped head would look great with Le Corbusier-style frames.

"No, no, Laura, I can't do glasses."

He's having trouble facing the inevitability of passing time. And yet you'd never realize it by seeing his nervous vitality, or by looking at him. He has just shot a video for an event organized by the Gelinaz (the extravagant gastronomic collective founded by journalist Andrea Petrini), in which he dives off the roof of the restaurant and into the lake. He smiles.

"Oh, that. It was a spur of the moment thing."

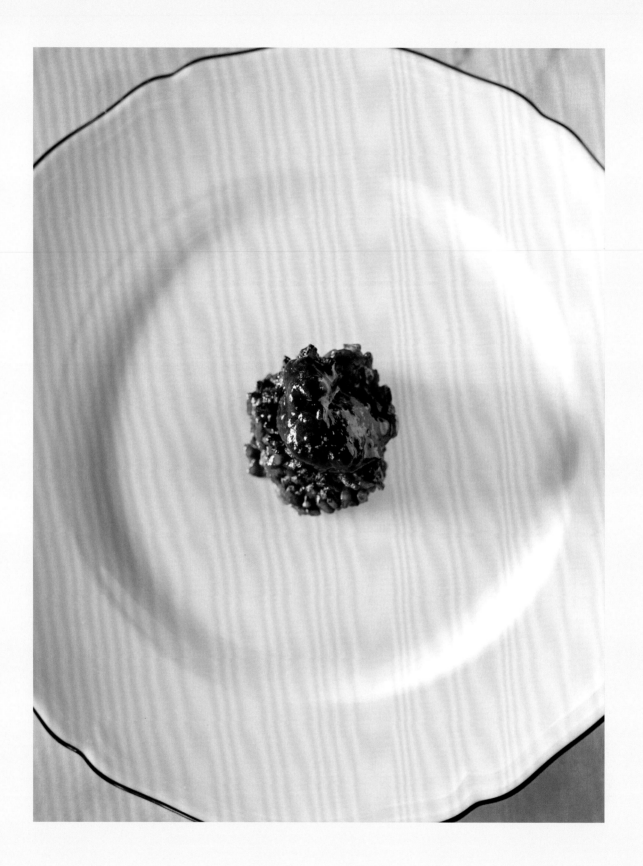

Riso Riscaldato
Reheated Rice

Riccardo Camanini was inspired to remake a dish he famously hated when he was a schoolchild (the reheated tomato rice served at his kindergarten cafeteria) by the discovery of an exceptional tomato paste made in big terracotta jugs by a Sicilian friend. The serving size is small (the flavor being particularly intense), so consider this an antipasto.

Tomato-infused olive oil (recipe follows)
½ cup Carnaroli or Arborio rice
Salt
2 tablespoons best-quality tomato paste
4 pitted prunes
2 tablespoons red vermouth
Ground Sansho Japanese pepper, to taste
4 basil leaves

Makes 4 small servings

Fill a small saucepan with water and bring it to a boil over high heat; add 1 tablespoon salt and adjust flame to maintain a steady simmer. Heat 2 tablespoons of tomato-infused olive oil in a medium-sized saucepan over medium heat. Add the rice and cook, stirring constantly with a wooden spoon, until opaque, 3 to 4 minutes. Sprinkle with a generous pinch of salt and stir in a half ladleful of boiling water. Cook, stirring often, until water is mostly absorbed, 2 to 3 minutes. Continue adding water, a half ladleful at a time, and stirring until absorbed. Adjust heat to medium-low as needed, to keep the risotto at a bare simmer. Cook, stirring often, until rice is just tender but still al dente. Remove from heat, stir in 2 tablespoons tomato-infused olive oil, 2 tablespoons tomato paste, and salt to taste.

Line a small baking sheet with parchment paper. Spoon the risotto into 4 small mounds on the tray and refrigerate until cold; about 1 hour, up to overnight.

Combine the prunes, vermouth and ground Sansho pepper in a blender or food processor and blend until smooth, set aside.

Preheat oven to 425°F. Transfer the risotto from the refrigerator directly into hot oven and bake for 10 minutes, or until the surface is toasted. Remove from oven, and transfer each mound of risotto to a warm plate. Top with prune sauce, garnish with a basil leaf and serve immediately.

Tomato-infused olive oil
½ cup extra-virgin olive oil
¼ cup diced red onion
½ garlic clove
1 ½ tablespoons tomato paste

Makes ½ cup

Preheat oven to 175°F, or lowest heat setting. Pour oil into a small saucepan over medium heat. When oil is hot and shimmering, add onion and half garlic clove; sauté until onion in translucent, 5 to 7 minutes. Add tomato paste and stir to combine thoroughly. Remove from heat, spoon into a heatproof container and place in oven for 24 hours.

Remove from oven and filter through a fine mesh sieve, reserving oil.

ANTONIA KLUGMANN
DAVIDE CARANCHINI
GIANNI DEZIO
ISABELLA POTÌ
FLORIANO PELLEGRINO

FINE DINING CREATIVES

ANTONIA

KLUGMANN

The sisters are going at it.

One is clad in chef's whites, the other is wearing a long linen dress, slightly Victorian-looking. The resemblance is striking; both women have angular, elegant features and a tenacious gaze that shifts constantly between incensed and pleased.

Antonia Klugmann—the one in whites, owner and chef of one-Michelin-star restaurant L'Argine a Vencò, is in the midst of an animated discussion with Vittoria, her sister and right hand woman. It's the first argument I witness between the two and I can tell there have been many—and that they all end in laughter. Their bond is indestructible but they're both tempestuous and stubborn.

It started with Antonia walking in with a bloody apron.

"I'm sorry, I was deboning a lamb," she apologizes, although I know she is not really apologizing. Antonia takes pride in being able to do everything, in being tough and not shying away from any task, no matter how brutal or harrowing.

She returns with an immaculate apron and the new chef's jacket she had made to measure. "It looks like something out of *Star Trek's* costume department," says Vittoria.

Antonia says something unflattering about Vittoria's dress.

"Why do you clip my wings?" she then asks. "Your task is to steer me away when you see I'm in my *'Titanic* mode' and about to hit the iceberg. Other than that, just let me be."

Vittoria goes in for a hug.

"Can you keep all this joy to yourself, please? It's distracting," quips Antonia, while pulling away.

Then there is a riff about a dish and how it's being plated. Antonia is making a point about symmetry and how much she likes symmetrical stuff:

"Had I not become a chef, I would have been a photographer." Vittoria says "Right," to which Antonia replies:

"You're telling me I'm right the way you'd tell a crazy person you don't want to upset."

Antonia rolls her eyes, Vittoria laughs.

"We used to beat each other up when we were little," explains Antonia, "and I was always the one ending up with bruises." She shrugs, "she was taller!"

Antonia Klugmann is one of the most gifted chefs I know, though when I think of her the word that comes to mind first is "fire." Whenever I'm standing next to her I sense something burning under her skin, a steadfast, unwavering commitment to the craft that is all-consuming and necessary to her survival.

It did save her life, metaphorically speaking. Many years ago, Antonia was in a car accident. She had been working as a chef: the daughter of doctors and already a certified assistant sailing instructor, she had flirted with law school and then opted out, beginning a string of soul-crushing kitchen jobs.

Her employers (who must be feeling quite contrite now) kept telling her she wasn't cut out for a career at the stove, but these comments didn't discourage her. She kept working, filling the margins of her notebooks with ideas for flavor pairings: something inside her suggested she'd need them some day. She never told her executive chefs about those ideas; she knew her technique was lacking, but she also knew her life objective, and she had a strong sense of self. ("To this day I ask my chefs not to tell me their ideas for dishes. Their creativity, their point of view is something they need to keep to themselves and safeguard for the time they too will have their own kitchen.") Then came the car accident, not a serious one, but bad enough for doctors to prescribe bedrest for a while. For months afterwards, all she could do was tend a vegetable garden. And cook in her head.

Because she couldn't work, she practiced mentally, using her sense memory to recall actions, smells, textures, imagining a dish from start to finish. Antonia still cooks each dish in her head before she tries it out in the kitchen. The first time she explained this to me she was still the executive chef at Venissa, a boutique wine resort on the island of Mazzorbo in the Venetian lagoon, owned by the Bisol family.

That was the job that effectively put her on the map: she succeeded in retaining the restaurant's Michelin star, producing a strong cuisine that was as much a celebration of the local ecosystem as of her love for

discipline, the world of vegetables, and the space in between the obvious flavors. At Venissa she learned how to command a proper kitchen brigade, and she found the inner silence she needed to be able to create. She also found the resolve to make the dream she shared with her then-partner, Maître D' Romano De Feo, come true: opening a restaurant surrounded by nature at the border between Friuli and Slovenia. She found the perfect spot in Vencò, in the province of Gorizia.

Antonia is a frontier woman. Her family comes from Apulia and Emilia, and one of her grandfathers was Jewish, with Eastern European roots. She was born in Trieste, with a love for the disputed territory where so much Italian history was written, a land of World War I battles, fought around the river Isonzo, and undulating vineyards, where today the good wines of Collio and the rosa di Gorizia (a prized variety of pink chicory) are produced.

L'Argine is a low, long building, surrounded by one hectare of land, with orchards and several plots of greens. The back overlooks a vineyard, the property of the Felluga family, the front a tall levee. Almost everything that grows here, whether wild or domesticated, is used for the restaurant's dishes. Foraging and picking are done twice a day, even during the winter when the soil is frozen before eleven a.m. and after four p.m.

Vegetables are a serious matter here; they provide most of the alphabet and punctuation of Antonia's dishes, while the vocabulary comes from the unusual traditions of this border land, a land where influences from the Trieste Gulf, the Alps, and Eastern-Central Europe, where sweet, smoky and bitter mingle, producing dishes such as risotto with hop shoots or bladder campion, hearty fish soups, stews, and broths made with stale bread and less noble cuts of meat.

Antonia mixes all this with other things she's tried, tasted, and liked during her life. The Gnocchi di Rapa Rossa, Prugna e Rosa (gnocchi with red beets, plum, and rose, recipe on page 152), one of her signature dishes, is a good example of her inspiration and her execution.

Antonia prides herself on her technique, which is classic, strong, borderline obsessive-compulsive. She likes to cook with a Lyonnaise iron pan and there are tasks she doesn't like to delegate, if she thinks—which she often does—none of her chefs can tackle them the way she would (like preparing breakfast for the guests of the four rooms at L'Argine, which she still does personally). "Il mio modo di essere è una rottura di coglioni," she says, "I'm a ball-buster, a pain in the ass."

You can tell she enjoys explaining a particularly complex preparation—like the gnocchi's: "I have a thing for using fruit in first courses, and in savory dishes in general, which is typical of my region," and as she says this I think of another dish, cappelletti filled with boar in a plum broth, her take on the regional darling, plum-filled gnocchi, which subconsciously she used as the inspiration for this one. "I also have a soft spot for red beets, though everybody started using them and I found it extremely irritating: it's dangerous when a particular ingredient becomes too popular. I don't want to be influenced and I don't want people to think I'm doing the same things as others."

The gnocchi are made with potatoes soaked in a red beet extraction; they're served with a sauce also made from red beet extraction and butter, fermented red plum, and a plum gelatin made by hot-extracting plums and then air-drying the juice. The dish is finished off with a rose and hibiscus powder, and Jerusalem artichoke chips. "The combination of red beet and butter produces a white chocolate note, which to me was a bit trite, so I added the Jerusalem artichoke: it adds a dark chocolate flavor, making things much more interesting." This dish was born out of a burst of creativity, at the end of the first vacation Antonia had taken in years. "At the end of those days I had fifteen new dishes. I went back into the kitchen, explained to each station chef what his task was going to be and after four days of trials we had locked all fifteen dishes down. It was a first for me."

Antonia is a tough but fair leader. She knows who will perform well under pressure. She knows who will be a good forager and who has passion but not talent for picking herbs. She knows who can be trusted with boiling eel—which is nobody. (The recipe for her eel is twice as complex as the one for gnocchi—it involves a series of marinating/boiling steps with a combination of apple cider, apple juice, white wine, red wine vinegar, fermented red cabbage, and a reduced broth made with the eel's head and bones.) "I like to bring everyone to their limit," she says. Including herself; she acknowledges that having more people in the kitchen, as opposed to when it was just her with one helper, allows her to push a bit harder, to aim for more ambitious preparations.

(The same goes for the front of house. I remember going to L'Argine shortly after its opening, years ago: Romano was in bed with the flu and Antonia had to call in her sister to wait tables.)

A bigger staff is one of the benefits she got from her one season as a judge on *MasterChef Italia*, something she did with mixed feelings: it brought her more notoriety and it attracted more clients to L'Argine (which now is almost always fully booked), a vital boost for a country restaurant, but it was also a distraction. She quit after one year.

Since she returned from her television stint, Antonia has added a back room with a full glass wall to L'Argine. Basked in the new-found light pouring in from the Felluga vineyard, the restaurant's artisanal wood cabinetry, the muted sage green of the walls and the beautiful artworks by painter Romolo Bertini—an uncle of her mother's—appear to be almost vibrating.

Antonia has been working on expanding her plots and orchards, particularly focusing on heirloom varieties. There are apricot, cherry (sweet and sour), jujube, peach, apple, plum, and quince trees surrounding L'Argine. Herbs, berries, legumes, pumpkins, zucchini, beets, Swiss chard, cucumbers grow in the plots, and the seeds (nigella, sunflower, flax, zucchini, sesame) for the dish Semi, Amaranto e Girasole (Seeds, Amaranth, Sunflower, recipe on page 155) all come from there. "In the next ten years I see myself devoting more time to my orchard and my garden, as I expand my production of preserves, jams, compotes, and broths. Romano and I already make our own vinegars, vermouths, and grappe. I feel there is so much more to be done here: it could really benefit this area if we all started looking into fruit as an investment. It could be our new economy."

There's a book in the making: it will be Antonia's second (the first, published during the *MasterChef* year, is an autobiography) and it will explore the issue of creativity: How do technical awareness and creativity feed off each other? Does having a richer vocabulary foster or clip the way the mind works?

She'll think about it while she remodels the barn adjoining L'Argine. Connected to the restaurant, it will boast two more guest rooms, and possibly Antonia's new house. I ask her if it's wise to live so close to her job.

"I am always here anyway. Even my phone knows it: when I drive to L'Argine in the morning Siri asks: "Are you going home?" I think Siri is confused," she laughs.

Gnocchi di Rapa Rossa, Prugna e Rosa
Beet Gnocchi with Plum Gelatin and Rose

This dish puts a contemporary spin on the use of fruit in savory courses, quite common in the "frontier" cuisine of Friuli (one of the local staples is a dish of plum-filled gnocchi) but, as in most of Antonia Klugmann's dishes, it takes it to a whole other level of complexity. Because of the difficulty of this recipe, you will need to weigh the quantities of beets and potato for the gnocchi dough, to assure you have the correct proportions. (Hibiscus powder can be bought online or in specialty food stores.)

5 medium–small beets
1 medium Russet potato
1 large egg
Salt, to taste
1 cup plus 3 tablespoons all-purpose flour
2 tablespoons butter, divided
Jerusalem artichoke chips (recipe follows)
Plum gelatin strips (recipe follows)
Hibiscus powder

Special equipment:
Steamer basket
Potato ricer or masher
Cold press juicer
Kitchen scale

Serves 2 to 4

Peel one of the beets, and slice very thinly, weighing the slices until you have 4.5 oz. of sliced beet. Similarly, peel and slice the potato, until you have 4.5 oz.. Reserve any remaining beet and potato for another use. Insert steamer basket into the bottom of a large pot. Fill with about 1 inch of water, making sure that the water level is just below the steamer basket. Add the sliced beets and potatoes to the basket and cover pot with a tight fitting lid. Bring water to a boil over high heat, then reduce to a simmer. Cook until vegetables are tender, 25 to 30 minutes.

Pass hot vegetables through a potato ricer into a large bowl (you may want to cover the bowl and ricer with a large dishcloth to avoid splatters). Add egg and ½ teaspoon salt. Mix with a wooden spoon just until the dough comes together. Stir in the flour until completely absorbed, and dough is soft and smooth. Do not over-work the dough; it will remain soft and sticky.

Divide dough into 4 equal portions; using your hands, transfer one of the portions onto a generously floured work surface. Gently mold into a log about 1 inch wide, and cut crosswise into ½ inch pieces. Repeat with remaining dough portions. Set aside gnocchi on a well-floured cutting board.

Juice the 4 remaining beets using a cold press juicer. Set aside ½ cup of the juice, and place the rest in a small saucepan over medium-high heat. Cook, maintaining a steady simmer, until the liquid has reduced considerably and becomes thick and syrupy, 30 to 35 minutes. Stir in 1 tablespoon butter until melted, and remove saucepan from heat.

Bring a large pot of water to a boil over high heat and add 3 tablespoons of salt. Gently transfer the gnocchi to the boiling water and cook until they float to the surface, 2 to 3 minutes. Meanwhile, melt 1 tablespoon of butter in a large frying pan or wok over medium-high heat. Using a slotted spoon, transfer the cooked gnocchi to the frying pan; add fresh beet juice and a pinch of salt and cook, shaking pan constantly, until liquid has thickened, 2 to 3 minutes. Pour in the reduced beet-butter sauce, shake pan to combine with beet juice, and remove from heat.

Divide the gnocchi between warm plates and top with a sprinkle of hibiscus powder. Crumble Jerusalem artichoke chips over the gnocchi and garnish with plum gelatin strips. Serve immediately.

Jerusalem Artichoke Chips
1 large Jerusalem artichoke
Canola oil, for frying

Preheat oven to 350°F. Wash and dry the Jerusalem artichoke; wrap tightly in aluminum foil. Cook the Jerusalem artichoke in hot oven until it is soft when poked with a sharp knife, about 30 minutes. Reduce oven temperature to 150°F.

Peel the Jerusalem artichoke, reserving peel. Set aside the artichoke for another use and place the peel in a single layer on a parchment-lined baking sheet. Place in warm oven until dry, about 1 ½ hours. Remove from oven and set aside to cool.

Heat about two inches of canola oil in a deep-frying pan until the oil sputters when you toss in a breadcrumb. When the oil is hot, add the Jerusalem artichoke peel, and fry until golden. Transfer to a paper-towel lined plate to dry. Sprinkle with salt, and keep warm.

Plum Gelatin Strips
Because of the high pectin content, this gelatin doesn't melt when it comes in contact with the warm gnocchi, therefore maintaining its shape and beautifully wrapping around them. Antonia makes her gelatin with a steam juicer, which is the ideal appliance to use for a perfect result. Cooking the fruit on the stovetop to extract the juice, as is done in this recipe, while effective, yields slightly thicker and more opaque strips than the ones Antonia serves in her restaurant.

4 lbs. fresh red plums, quartered and pitted

Place plum pieces in a medium saucepan, add 1 tablespoon of water, cover, and cook over low heat until the plums have released most of their juice, 30 to 35 minutes. Filter with a fine mesh sieve to a small saucepan and reserve solids for another use.

Place saucepan over medium heat and bring to a boil. Cook, stirring occasionally until juice has reduced by about half, 25 to 30 minutes.

Preheat oven to 175°F and line a rimmed 11x17-inch jellyroll pan or sheetpan with sides with parchment paper. Pour the mixture into the prepared pan and cook in preheated oven until dry to touch, about 3 hours. Remove from oven, let cool, and peel the sheet off the parchment paper. Transfer to a cutting board and cut into very small, irregularly-shaped strips.

Semi, Amaranto e Girasole
Seeds, Amaranth, Sunflower

Make sure the cucumber and zucchini you're using are very ripe in order to be able to extract their seeds. The seeds of other vegetables can be used, depending on the time of the year, as this dish—healthy and hearty, with a texture reminiscent of grits—is one of Antonia Klugmann's odes to seasonal vegetables.

2/3 cup (3.5 oz.) raw sunflower seeds
1 pinch of sugar
Salt
2 tablespoons sunflower oil
1 ripe cucumber with seeds
1 ripe zucchini
2 cups water
½ cup (3.5 oz.) amaranth grain
Extra virgin olive oil
1 tablespoon flax seeds
1 tablespoon black caraway (nigella sativa) seeds
1 teaspoon poppy seeds
½ tablespoon white sesame seeds
½ tablespoon black sesame seeds

Serves 4

Place the sunflower seeds in a small bowl and cover with cold water. Let soak for 45 minutes. Strain seeds and pat dry with paper towels.

Preheat oven to 350°F. Spread sunflower seeds in a single layer on a parchment-lined baking sheet and cook until fragrant and lightly toasted, about 10 to 12 minutes. Let cool slightly. Transfer the seeds to a blender; add a pinch of sugar, a pinch of salt and sunflower oil. Blend into a smooth, thick paste. Add more oil if necessary to reach the desired consistency.

Slice zucchini and cucumber in half lengthwise; extract the seeds and with a small spoon. Transfer seeds and attached pulp to a fine mesh sieve and rinse thoroughly. Pat seeds dry with paper towels and set aside; reserve the zucchini and cucumber for another use.

Bring 2 cups water to a boil in a small saucepan over high heat. When the water boils, add the amaranth and stir to combine. Return to a boil, then lower heat to maintain a steady simmer. Cook for 20 to 22 minutes, stirring with a wooden spoon, occasionally at first and more frequently towards the end of cooking time, until all the water has been absorbed, and the amaranth has assumed the consistency of polenta. Stir in a pinch of salt and 2 teaspoons of olive oil until well combined. Set aside.

Heat a heavy, cast-iron skillet over medium heat. Add flax seeds, black caraway, poppy seeds, and both types of sesame seeds to the hot pan and cook, stirring often until seeds are fragrant and toasted, about 3 to 5 minutes. Transfer seeds to a plate and set aside.

Spread a spoonful of sunflower seed paste into a circle in the center of a serving plate, then cover with a ladleful of cooked amaranth. Garnish with toasted seed mix and raw cucumber and zucchini seeds. Serve immediately.

DAVIDE

CARANCHINI

One would think Davide Caranchini isn't the type to open up about personal details. A massive guy, with an almost fixed frown, he comes across as a bit cagey, even aloof. But get him to talk about his cuisine (or the soccer rivalry between the towns of Como and Varese) and he will warm up immediately.

Caranchini, with wife Ambra Sberna and her brothers Luca and Marco, owns Materia, a one-Michelin-star restaurant in Cernobbio. It is largely thanks to this small, unassuming restaurant and its cult following that this quaint town on Lake Como has become known for something other than the magnificent Villa Erba, or its proximity to George Clooney's summer estate.

The restaurant is tiny, but Caranchini maintains a large greenhouse, with more than a hundred varieties of herbs and vegetables. A broccoli fanatic since kindergarten (his grandparents had a vegetable garden), Caranchini used to eat not just his own vegetables, but also those of his friends. "I have always loved and respected vegetables," he says. "But I didn't always see them as central to a dish." An early culinary vagabondism took him from his native Cernobbio to London, where he worked at Le Gavroche and Apsleys. "For the classically-trained French, vegetables play a supporting role at best. Only when I worked my way to Noma, in Copenhagen, did I realize it was possible to rethink the way we use them."

He returned from his experience abroad with a fresh point of view on something he had cherished all along. "At Materia we grow all kinds of root vegetables, and between our own production and the supplies we get from two organic local farms, we're a hundred percent self-sufficient." Caranchini now treats vegetables as if they were animal protein.

Case in point is his daikon in carpione (his version of the traditional marinade is made with tosazu, a bonito-flavored rice vinegar and lemon olive oil), topped with tempura and pickled shallot. It has a quasi-meaty texture.

"Carpione is one of those recipes one immediately associates with lake cuisine. I draw from the French for the basics, but I think I have a certain freshness, a clean kind of approach I learned at Noma. Having said this, my main source of inspiration is my surroundings. I like the lake because it maintains a very peculiar geographic and cultural ecosystem."

He's unusually articulate and precise, both with words and dishes, for someone so young; he also has a distinctive culinary voice, something one wouldn't immediately expect from a recently fledged talent. What struck me the first time I tried his food was the flavor palette, which is far from your usual "round/sweet with a touch of acidity" or "badass bitter."

Caranchini does acidic and bitter nicely, but he mostly likes to play with the multifaceted spectrum of fermentation-related flavors; when I suggest that this is more of an acquired taste for Italians, he disagrees: "Oh, I actually think fermentation is something we've known all long and we're pretty comfortable with. Fermented foods are the norm on the mountains and on lakes."

If you think about it, the ancient Romans used the process, too (the fermented fish sauce known as garum is not an invention of the Nordics). "Rancid"—a flavor that partly overlaps, in a favorable way, with fermented— is the term that came to mind when I tried Davide's exceptional, paper-thin fresh pasta buttons filled with fermented potato (of the low-starch Biancona di Como variety) and served on a rye curd, with a sourdough levain foam, chive oil, and smoked herring caviar. "We lacto-ferment the potato in a two-percent salt brine, until its pH reaches five points. I loved the idea of using rye, because that's what we eat here: rice, barley, rye, not pasta." (When rye is sprouted and fermented, and then heated with milk and alpine pasture cream, it acts as a clotting agent, like lemon juice.) "Chive oil and herring roe provide aromatic and smoky notes that go very well with potatoes: think of potatoes and onions, or ash-roasted potatoes."

I ate that dish and detected an unusual flavor I was familiar with, but couldn't quite place. "The same happens to a lot of locals who come eat here—like when they try dishes like my version of *missoltino*. They eat something they've never had before, yet they lock into a flavor they've known all their lives."

Every household on the lago di Como has made *missoltino*. It's prepared with agone, a slim lake fish which is caught in moderation (its population is dwindling) and in a short season: in June and July they keep near the bottom of the lake as they lay their eggs, so the few fishermen still investing in this niche product look for them around September, when they swim closer to the surface. Scaling and deboning agone is a painstaking job: its bones are tiny and brittle. The locals have long had the habit of salt-drying agone in the sun, before washing and canning it. (Says Caranchi: "It basically ferments as it dries, and in doing so it develops a peculiar flavor not everyone has the stomach for: if you feed it to ten people, eight won't like it.")

Caranchini uses fresh agone. He barbecues it and serves it with a sauce made with fermented white asparagus and a broth of fish bones and heads, topped with fresh wood sorrel. It comes with two separate

sides: avocado and agone roe, sprinkled with ceviche (also made with the agone roe), and lettuce hearts served with a lettuce extraction and a mayonnaise of agone garum. "It's an agone that wants to speak to the world!" jokes Davide.

Dining at Materia, as in so many other fine dining restaurants in Italy, means choosing between the tasting menu and dining à la carte. "If it was up to me I'd only do tasting. But à la carte is a commercial compromise I have to make: we're still in the process of proving ourselves and I can't afford to lose our regulars."

An argument can be made for freedom: we should all be able to order what we want, especially if we're already familiar with a restaurant's signature cuisine. There is also the point that not all chefs know how to edit themselves, and many tasting menus end up being almost rambling.

Yet an opposite argument can be made for an author's right to direct his own movie: a tasting menu is the most efficient and cohesive way for chefs to show their range and approach. It's also efficient from the point of view of kitchen organization: only a certain number of lines have to be ready every night. Most fine dining chefs in Italy still choose to offer both options, like Caranchini.

I can vouch for Caranchini's tasting menus: they might be long (from five to eleven courses), but they're not rambling. Take his petit fours, something I vehemently wish to see abolished from all establishments

(along with amuse-bouches): Caranchini's version of these end of meal treats are chanterelles that have been candied in honey and fermented for a month, coca leaves and mini tarts made with ancient grains and eucalyptus. They show a genuine attempt at being both subtle and titillating. Then there are his desserts.

I personally think desserts should either be tightly connected to the savory part of the meal (something Romito has been advocating), or break completely with it, in which case they should reflect our history and palate. What they shouldn't be is generic: quenelles, crumbles, and syrupy drippings still seem to be the choice of too many chefs. I find this lazy and disappointing, at best.

Which is why I like Caranchini's decision (somewhat reminiscent of what Riccardo Camanini does at Lido 84) to stick to classics, like baba and crostata. He even has a dessert inspired by Risotto Allo Zafferano (recipe on page 163), the Milanese classic saffron risotto. "If you can't be truly innovative, you should probably do what you know best," he says, and I couldn't agree more.

Midollo e Zafferano, Omaggio a Milano
Bone Marrow and Saffron, Homage to Milan

Though the ingredients in this recipe might hint at a more cerebral dessert, Caranchini's sweet take on risotto allo zafferano is luscious and deeply satisfying, both in texture and flavor. It will come as no surprise, however, that due to the bone marrow and the large quantity of saffron, this dessert is easily the most expensive dish in the book!

Saffron Whipped Cream
2 cups heavy cream
1 tablespoon packed saffron threads
1/3 cup plus 2 tablespoons powdered sugar
A pinch of salt

Filo Disks
1 sheet filo pastry
2 teaspoons clarified marrow (recipe follows), melted
1 teaspoon powdered sugar

To finish
4 scoops bone marrow gelato (recipe follows)
1 teaspoon finely grated lemon zest
1/4 cup clarified marrow (recipe follows), frozen solid

Special equipment:
3 ½ or 4-inch round cookie cutter
Immersion blender
Ice cream maker

Serves 4

For the saffron whipped cream
Heat ¼ cup heavy cream in a small saucepan over medium heat, until steaming; do not bring to a boil. Remove from heat, add saffron threads, and set aside to steep at room temperature, about 30 minutes. Combine the saffron-infused cream with the rest of the cream in a glass container, cover, and refrigerate overnight.

The next day, strain the saffron cream through a fine mesh sieve (discard used saffron threads) and combine it with the powdered sugar and a pinch of salt in a large bowl. Whip cream into soft peaks and chill until ready to serve.

For the filo disks
Preheat oven to 400°F. Unroll the sheet of filo pastry on a cutting board and, using a 3 ½ or 4-inch round cookie cutter, cut out 4 rounds of pastry. Transfer rounds to a parchment-lined baking sheet, brush with melted clarified marrow and sprinkle with powdered sugar. Bake in hot oven until sugar is caramelized and disks are golden, 6 to 7 minutes. Remove from oven and set aside to cool at room temperature.

To finish
Prepare 4 serving plates; place a scoop of gelato in the middle of each plate, and top generously with saffron whipped cream and

¼ teaspoon grated lemon zest. Cover with the filo disk and use a sharp, small-holed grater to grate the frozen marrow over the top of each dessert. Serve immediately.

Bone Marrow Gelato
2 cups whole milk
1/3 cup powdered milk
1/3 cup plus 2 tablespoons heavy cream
1 tablespoon corn syrup
¾ cup granulated sugar
¼ cup plus 2 tablespoons clarified marrow (recipe follows), melted

Combine milk, powdered milk, heavy cream, corn syrup, and sugar in a heavy-bottomed saucepan over medium-low heat. Bring to a simmer, stirring often, then remove from heat and cool to room temperature. Add the melted marrow and blend on high speed with an immersion blender to combine thoroughly.

Pour mixture immediately into ice cream maker (do not refrigerate first, or the mixture will separate) and churn according to manufacturers' instructions. Transfer ice cream to an airtight container and chill in freezer until ready to serve.

Clarified Bone Marrow
Two 7-inch sections of center-cut beef marrow bone (ask your butcher to halve them lengthwise for you)

Makes about ¾ cup clarified marrow

Carefully extract the marrow from the bone with a spoon and a small, sharp knife. Break the marrow into small pieces and place in the top of a double boiler over barely simmering water. Cook over very low heat, stirring occasionally, until marrow melts completely, about 20 minutes. Strain through a fine mesh sieve into a bowl.

GIANNI

DEZIO

I have seen many cathedrals in my life, but few rival the beauty of the Basilica di Santa Maria Assunta, in Atri. Built in the Abruzzese Romanesque style, with a weirdly harmonious facade (an immense rectangle, unadorned save for an arresting rose window and a gothic portal), it is one of the signature landmarks of this region.

A short drive from the cathedral there's another masterpiece: the *calanchi* (ravines) of Atri's World Wildlife Fund nature reserve: clayey/sandy hills chiseled by water over hundreds of years and dotted by emerald green vegetation. On a clear day, you can see the Adriatic Sea behind them. No matter where you are, the beautiful opus of man and nature are intertwined in Abruzzo.

Gianni Dezio was born here. His restaurant is close to the cathedral and he often picks herbs (mint, fennel, purslane) in the fields surrounding the *calanchi*—he even represented them in a dessert, an edible landscape that mimics their shape. Art and plants imbue his cuisine. "Wild licorice used to grow abundantly in this area," he tells me, "which is why Atri is the home of Menozzi De Rosa, the largest licorice manufacturer in Italy. When I was little I would catch whiffs of licorice coming from the factory; the whole town smelled like it."

Licorice is one of Tosto's signature ingredients: it appears at the very beginning of the meal, in the house grissini; it's also prominently displayed in a lamb sirloin dish: the meat is skewered on dried licorice root and glazed with gravy made with lamb jus and licorice paste. Gianni's sommelier wife Daniela, who cares for the tables of their thirty-seat restaurant, pairs it with a saffron-infused gin and tonic.

Most of Gianni's dishes are like this: elegant and tasty, but not obvious. Take the gnocchi with seaweed, razor clams, and pine nut sauce (almonds seem to be all the rage and I'm always happy when I find pine nuts used instead); or the tagliolini with lardo, cuttlefish, and rosemary extract (page 169), a nice play on textures and color gradients. "I like working with ingredients that bridge the sea and the hills," says Gianni. "And I like working on a dish until it feels perfect to me: I'm not interested in improvising and starting from scratch every few weeks."

Gianni is firm but soft-spoken and he knows how to listen. He's meditative and refreshingly devoid of smartass genes. His cuisine is a compendium of the best elements of this specific area and of his own background: Though originally from Atri, Gianni lived between Italy and Venezuela for most of his youth. He moved to a town called Calabozo, in Venezuela, after graduating from high school and opened a restaurant there with his family. But he longed for his homeland and eventually came back for culinary school. "I was torn between Alma and Niko Romito's culinary school. I chose the latter because it was in Abruzzo."

Romito makes no mystery of considering Gianni one of his best students. Gianni, who was part of the class that opened the first Spazio (page 22), was the first alumnus to have a restaurant of his own. And Dezio's approach to ingredients—restrained, balanced, flavor-driven—is a testament to his apprenticeship under the three-Michelin-star chef. "At the beginning my cuisine was very much derivative of Spazio's. But I set out to find my own voice."

166

Gianni's contemporary Abruzzese cuisine is carefully contaminated. You won't find any arepas on his menu ("I try not to remake traditional Venezuelan dishes, rather to use ingredients that are functional to my cuisine, like coriander, passion fruit, and rum"), but his roots are clearly detectable in dishes like the hare served with a sauce made with burnt cane sugar, or the pumpkin ceviche.

Before Tosto, he and his wife (who is Italo-Venezuelan) drove around the region in search of small producers to work with. Abruzzo has a strong pastoral tradition so they followed the path of raw sheep's milk cheese, selecting the best pecorino. Next were honey, saffron, and local charcuterie-like ventricina, a spicy spreadable sausage Dezio turns into a butter-like paste and serves with homemade bread. Seafood comes from nearby Giulianova, spirits from local small-batch distilleries, like L-AB, (Liquoreria Abruzzese), the producer of a notable line of gentian-based liquors. "And we're going to start working with the farmers from Azienda Agricola Vallese: they are the first to farm rice in Abruzzo in a very long time."

Working as a restaurateur in a small town doesn't bother him, but having a small restaurant does. Gianni and Daniela's next challenge will be finding a space as big as their ambitions. Will it still be in Abruzzo? "You bet it will."

Tagliolini di Acqua e Farina, Lardo, Seppia e Rosmarino
Tagliolini with Lardo, Cuttlefish, and Rosemary

Though fresh pasta is usually associated with the north of Italy, this humble version, made with just flour and water, can also be found in the center and south, both traditionally dry pasta territory. At Tosto, Gianni Dezio's mother is in charge of making the pasta, though the idea of pairing these tagliolini with both lardo and cuttlefish (almost indistinguishable in color) and finishing off with rosemary extract is Gianni's, and relies on the balance and contrast of nuances (a jolt of green against a gradient of whites) and textures (melting and crunchy).

¾ cup (3.5 oz.) all-purpose flour
⅔ cup (3.5 oz.) semolina flour
½ cup hot water
2 cups prosciutto broth (recipe follows)
1 clove of garlic, peeled
¼ teaspoon cayenne pepper
1 lb. cuttlefish, cleaned and rinsed
4.5 oz. Lardo di Colonnata
1 tablespoon extra-virgin olive oil
4 tablespoons rosemary extract (recipe follows)

Special equipment:
Stand Mixer
Pasta Machine

Serves 4

Stir together the flour and semolina in the bowl of a stand mixer fitted with a dough hook (or a large bowl, if mixing by hand) to create a mound with a crater in the center. Pour the water into the crater and use the dough hook (or your fingers) on low speed to gradually mix the dough until it comes together in a crumbly mass. Knead on medium-low speed for 7 minutes until the dough is very smooth and elastic. If it is sticky, knead in a teaspoon of flour at a time until it doesn't stick to your hands when touched. Tightly wrap the dough in plastic wrap and allow it to relax in the refrigerator for 20 to 30 minutes.

Remove dough from refrigerator and discard plastic wrap. Cut the dough into two pieces and flatten each piece into a rough rectangle. Lightly dust the rollers of a pasta machine with all-purpose flour and pass one piece of dough through the machine on the largest setting. Fold the dough in thirds and pass through the rollers again. Continue rolling the dough through the machine, dusting with semolina flour as necessary and adjusting to a smaller setting each time, until the sheet is thin, about 2 mm. Dust pasta sheet generously with flour; fold in half, dust with flour again, fold, and repeat, until you have a 3-inch roll of pasta. Cut roll crosswise into thin strips, creating long, thin tagliolini noodles. Shake the noodles apart and place on a clean kitchen towel; dust lightly with flour.

Combine the broth, garlic, and cayenne pepper in a wide, deep skillet over medium-high heat. Bring to a boil, then simmer until the liquid is thick and shiny, about 10 minutes.

Meanwhile bring a large pot of water to a boil over high heat. Remove the cuttlefish tentacles and reserve them for a different use. Slice the cuttlefish mantles and lardo into thin strips the same width as the pasta. Add 3 tablespoons of salt to the boiling water, then toss in the fresh pasta. Cook the noodles for about 20 seconds. Strain, then transfer pasta to the pan with the reduced broth. Cook over high heat for until broth is absorbed, shaking the pan constantly, about 20 seconds. Remove from heat and add 1 tablespoon extra-virgin olive oil, cuttlefish, and lardo strips; mix well to combine. Divide the pasta between 4 warm plates and drizzle with rosemary extract. Serve immediately.

Prosciutto Broth
This recipe was designed to use all the parts of prosciutto crudo that usually end up in the trash: the skin, excess fat, and bone. Ask a butcher who carries prosciutto crudo if he will hold onto these pieces for you, or (in a pinch) you can make the broth out of prosciutto crudo itself instead of the scraps.

16 oz. prosciutto scraps (skin, fat, bone)
4 cups cold water

Combine prosciutto scraps and cold water in a medium saucepan over medium-high heat. Bring to a boil, and immediately reduce heat to maintain a steady, gentle simmer. Simmer uncovered for 3 hours. Set aside to cool, skim fat off surface, then filter through a fine mesh sieve or cheesecloth.

Rosemary Extract
If you don't have a juicer, you can blend the rosemary needles in a blender with half a cup of ice water on very high speed until smooth. Let stand for fifteen minutes, then filter through a fine mesh sieve. However, the result will be less flavorful than the juiced version.

2 lbs. fresh rosemary needles

Special equipment:
Cold press juicer

Rinse the rosemary needles and place them in a large bowl, cover with cold water and ice cubes and refrigerate for 12 hours. Remove rosemary from refrigerator and strain in a colander. Extract juice from rosemary using a cold press juicer. Store juice in refrigerator until ready to use.

ISABELLA POTÌ

& FLORIANO PELLEGRINO

Love or hate: there is no in between when talking about the couple Potì/Pellegrino. I have yet to meet a more polarizing duo in Italian cuisine; people think either they're geniuses or that they're the product of a well-oiled hype machine. In full courtroom style I will simply present the facts and let you draw your own conclusions. I will say this, though: they're a quite unique phenomenon, one that can't possibly be ignored.

First off, if this chapter were an episode of a Netflix show, I'd recommend you watch it in Italian, with subtitles. Not being able to hear Floriano Pellegrino's original words is a substantial loss: so much of his character is reflected in his speech. Husky voice, distinct Apulian accent, a most noticeable mix of Italian and English. Rated R. Here's an example of one of his lines, presented as he delivered it:

"Dobbiamo spaccare i culi: perché uno da fucking New York e tutti i fucking giornalisti around the world dovrebbero venire qua?" (We must be kicking ass: otherwise, why should anyone from fucking New York and all the fucking journalists from around the world come all the way here?).

Is he a foul-mouthed, fully-tattooed, thug-life-loving millennial (he's thirty, Isabella in her mid-twenties) with an ego problem? Maybe so, but he's also one of the hardest working people I know, punctual, smart, and studious, very good at reading his surroundings and acting accordingly (even if it means losing the swear words). He's a team player and a leader, with a knack for riling his crew up. He plays rugby and draws from sports for his pep talks: "Pass the ball back to move forward."

Isabella and Floriano share the same drive: she speaks five languages, she's shy but firm, and incredibly polite. Her voice is even smokier than her partner's; she's beautiful, with impossibly high cheekbones and porcelain skin. She's unconsciously sultry and ironic. An unintentional diva.

Together, they run Bros', a one-Michelin-star restaurant in the historic center of Lecce, and Roots, a trattoria in Scorrano, where they live, a small, not at all picturesque town outside Lecce, one of those alienating places smart kids can't wait to get the hell away from. They call it, ironically and defiantly, "Scorrangeles". Floriano was born in Lecce, while Isabella was born in Rome, half "Salentina," half Polish.

They traveled far from home as soon as they could: Floriano spent a few years in the Basque country, mainly at the three-Michelin-star restaurant of Martín Berasategui, the man he considers his mentor. He absorbed the older man's laser focus and unwavering discipline, and he transferred them to his restaurant. Martín comes up often in conversation with Floriano. "He believed in us, even in the beginning when we didn't have money. He offered to send us dishes and glasses . . . I'm tearing up just remembering it." Isabella, who specialized in pastry, worked at Claude Bosi's, Mauro Colagreco's, and Paco Torreblanca's.

Bros' was initially conceived as a family project: it opened with two of the three Pellegrino brothers (hence the name), Floriano and Giovanni (Francesco, a pastry chef, wasn't part of it). Something didn't work out (Floriano doesn't like talking about it, though the industry grapevine has all sorts of theories) and Giovanni left, replaced by Isabella. She began as sous chef and was then promoted to head chef, with Floriano acting as executive chef and supervisor of all the Bros' sister projects (they're co-owners of the restaurant).

Part of Bros' mystique is its unclear power dynamic: some say Isabella is the one who develops dishes, others that Floriano is the real master; he calls her his "muse." When they're together he does most of the talking. Magicians don't share their tricks as it might take away from the magic. "Bros' is fine dining for millennials. Millennials are the ones who will make up most of restaurants' customer base in the coming years."

Brash, perhaps. But he does have a point. Bros' is the perfect bridge between Michelin and a young, opinionated crowd with spending power, taste, and a sense of adventure. It's not just a restaurant with the stated mission to "explore a flavor bedrock that can't be reduced to stereotypes," specifically that of Salento, the southernmost part of Apulia. It's also a carefully coordinated corporate image, an e-commerce business with branded jerseys, caps, and iPhone cases, videos, commercial deals (Isabella developed a limited-edition Cornetto gelato for Algida), a rugby team. The staff takes improv, speech, and English classes; they all have access to a life coach.

"We approach every menu change as if we were in the fashion or music business: we update our merchandise, shoot a new video, replace the front of house uniforms and even change the color of the restaurant's sign." Upon leaving the restaurant, customers are handed a balloon with the restaurant's logo: a smart way to make them ambassadors as they walk back to their car or their hotel.

All these products and experiences fall under the umbrella of "Metaprogetto," a metaphoric control room run by a strategy officer and Floriano. Future plans include a line of jarred sauces, a snazzy B&B (Bros' House—yes, after Soho House). There's also the dream of taking over masseria Pellegrino, Floriano's family agriturismo. (At the time of our conversation, he hadn't talked to his mother in a while: though he's not completely estranged from his family, there's clearly some feud to be squashed.)

A change of menu at Bros' involves calling up a team of experts including Floriano's uncle and a Salentine gastronomist: new dishes are sampled and judged based on the veracity of their flavors. The starting point is the taste of Salento, adjusted to represent each "microseason" and dressed in a form that is precise, contemporary, and playful. Though dishes are not always wholly original (mostly betraying Floriano's Spanish and Isabella's French periods, and the fact that they follow closely the work of heavyweights like Romito), they are sharp and entertaining.

Let's start with desserts. While texturally attracted by soufflés (which she gracefully serves kneeling table-side, in a pretty theatrical and I must say commanding moment), île flottants, and quenelles, Isabella has been working in vegetables, fermentation, and pickles. "We've always used them," she says during one of Floriano's rare pauses. "Our first soufflé was with celery; we made a rhubarb, malt, and buttermilk dessert; we also use a lot of beetroot, lately paired with an interesting pomegranate molasses."

Game dishes prove they can be technically astute, fish courses betray a tendency to swing between playful and restrained. A simple grilled monkfish with string beans was one my favorite dishes overall. Their beautiful *timballo di pasta*, *gambero e prezzemolo* (a spaghetti flan filled with shrimp and served in a parsley soup) draws from the perpetual dualism of southern cuisines, caught between the highbrow and the popular.

Semi di Pomodoro, *Colatura di Alici e Vaniglia* (tomato seeds, anchovy sauce, and vanilla) while reminiscent of a famous Josean Alija's tomato dish, has a pretty convincing genesis: the need to repurpose kitchen-prep waste (the seeds), the memory of *frisella con pomodoro* (a typical dried rustic bread, usually served with juicy toppings), a love for extra virgin olive oil (one of the region's chief products), a taste for unctuosity, acidity, and astringency. Then there's the *Spaghetto Aglio*, *Grasso Rancido*, *Peperoncino* (recipe on page 176), arguably their signature dish, a sensational take on spaghetti with garlic, oil, and red peppers, in which the oil is replaced with a salsa rancida.

"Il gusto per il rancido ce l'abbiamo inside," Rancid (referring to something pungent, like oxidized meat fat, and used by most Italian chefs with a positive connotation) is an innate flavor for us, says Floriano. "Take my nonna: she belongs to a generation that used commercial bouillons in the kitchen, who was coming of age when the quick and easy appeal of chemistry was taking over the poetry of the hearth. But she has always preferred rancid oil made from olives that have fallen from the tree."

There is nothing Floriano and Isabella hate more than being provincial, and they're not wrong when they wish Italy, particularly the lesser-known regions of the center and south, did a better job at presenting itself to an international public. Most of Bros' clientele comes from abroad; their kitchen brigade is predominantly non-Italian; Yuta Bise, the head chef of Roots trattoria, where all food is cooked in an old wood fire oven, is from Okinawa. "Because we needed a young Japanese man to show us the value of a zucchini cooked as simply as possible."

Floriano would like to turn Salento into a year-round destination. He would like it to be "the California of Italy."

Maybe he'll make this happen. "You can't build a skyscraper if all you think of is a shotgun shack."

Spaghetto, Aglio, Grasso Rancido, Peperoncino
Spaghetti with Garlic, Rancid Fat, and Crushed Chiles

The term rancid pinpoints a very specific flavor, which falls within the spectrum of fermentation. Chefs like Davide Caranchini (see page 156) and Francesco Capuzzo Dolcetta (see page 206) are comfortable around it, as it resonates with their memory of flavor. The same goes for Floriano Pellegrino and Isabella Potì: rancid notes reminds them of ricotta forte, a particularly pungent kind of ricotta typical of Salento, as well as of the salt used to pack anchovies. Their rancid fat sauce starts with a prosciutto bone broth which was a specialty of Basque chef Martín Berasategui, around the time Floriano worked with him. At Bros' it was initially used to glaze guinea fowl breasts. The duo then decided to use it for their take on aglio, olio e peperoncino which they serve cold; as they learned by eating countless servings of leftover pasta for breakfast, a cool serving temperature brings out the many layers of flavors in the dressing. It became so successful Floriano and Isabella decided to build a commercial range of jarred sauces around it. (When asking your butcher to reserve prosciutto bones for you, pick up an extra one for Gianni Dezio's recipe on page 169.) Note: Due to the richness of this pasta, the serving sizes are small, so both the Rancid Fat Sauce and Garlic Sauce recipes make more than you'll need for one pasta dish. Do not try to reduce the measurements or they won't properly emulsify. (Extra sauce can be stored in the refrigerator for up to a week.)

8 oz. spaghetti
2/3 cup Rancid Fat Sauce (recipe follows)
3 tablespoons Garlic Sauce (recipe follows)
Crushed red chiles, to taste
Salt

Bring a large pot of water to a boil over high heat and add 2 tablespoons of salt. Cook spaghetti until al dente. Drain, rinse under cold water, drain again, and transfer to a large bowl; add both sauces and toss to combine thoroughly. Divide pasta between 4 salad plates and sprinkle with crushed red chiles. Serve immediately.

Garlic Sauce
3 whole heads of garlic
3 cups milk
4 cups canola oil
Salt

Special Equipment:
Instant read thermometer
Immersion blender

Makes about 1 ½ cups

Separate garlic cloves; peel, halve, and remove the green germ from each clove. Place all of the garlic in a small saucepan and cover with 1 cup cold milk. Bring to a boil and then strain, discarding milk; return garlic to the pot. Cover with 1 cup cold milk and repeat previous steps twice, for a total of 3 times.

Place strained, blanched garlic in a clean saucepan and cover with 3 cups canola oil. Place over very low heat and test the temperature of the oil regularly, maintaining a temperature between 140°F to 148°F (you may have to remove the pot from the heat occasionally to avoid overheating). Cook at this temperature until garlic is soft, 35 to 40 minutes. Drain garlic cloves.

Place garlic cloves in the blender cup of an immersion blender. Begin blending on low speed and gradually add remaining cup of canola oil in a steady stream while blending continuously. Raise speed to medium-high and blend until creamy and fluffy. Add ¼ teaspoon salt, or more to taste.

Rancid Fat Sauce
1 lb. pork skin
1 large bone from a whole prosciutto crudo ham
1 tablespoon plus 1 teaspoon red wine vinegar
½ cup whole milk
3 ½ tablespoons reduced chicken stock, melted but not hot (recipe follows)
1 cup canola oil
Salt

Special equipment:
Immersion blender

Makes about 1 ½ cups

Combine pork skin and prosciutto bone in a large stockpot and cover with cold water. Bring to a boil over high heat; reduce to low heat and simmer gently for about 6 hours, until fat separates and comes to the surface. Filter through a fine mesh sieve into a tall jar or pitcher. Cover and refrigerate until set, 3 to 4 hours. The orange fat which rises to the top and solidifies, is the rancid fat. Scoop out 3 tablespoons of this fat, melt in a microwave on high for 30 to 45 seconds, then let cool slightly.

Pour into the blender jar of an immersion blender, one at a time in the following order: vinegar, milk, chicken stock, rancid fat, canola oil. Carefully insert the immersion blender to the very bottom of the jar and begin blending on slow speed, very slowly lifting up the blender as you go along, to incorporate all ingredients. Blend until mixture is light and creamy. Taste for salt, adding more if desired.

Reduced Chicken Stock
3 lbs. raw chicken parts (backs, wings, necks, bones)
Extra virgin olive oil

Makes about ¾ cup

Heat a tablespoon of extra virgin olive oil in the bottom of a large stockpot or Dutch oven. Working in batches, brown chicken parts in hot oil, turning occasionally, until golden, about 7 minutes. Return all the browned chicken parts to the pot and cover generously with cold water. Cook over very low heat, for 12 hours, without letting it boil. Filter the broth through a fine mesh sieve into a clean, small saucepan; discard solids. Bring broth to a boil over medium heat and cook until mixture has reduced by two thirds and has thickened considerably, 45 minutes to 1 hour (the desired texture should be similar to liquid honey: it should coat the back of a spoon). Let cool at room temperature before refrigerating.

Cocktail "Not So Fitness"
"Not So Fitness" Cocktail

**"It has plum juice, so you could pretend it's healthy," jokes
Floriano Pellegrino explaining the peculiar name of this cocktail,
"but then it has brandy, mezcal, and bergamot liqueur so, you
know, not so healthy, 'not so fitness!'" At Bros' it is typically
served to mark the transition from the acidic-dominant part of
the tasting menu, which means often right after the Spaghetti
with Garlic, Rancid Fat, and Crushed Chiles (recipe on page
176). Bergamot liqueur (especially of the brand Italicus) can be
found online or in specialty spirits shops. Orange powder may
also be bought online or made at home by grinding dehydrated
orange peel into a fine powder.**

4 oz. fresh plum juice
Scant 1 jigger (1 1/3 oz.) orange brandy, such as Orange Brandy by
Antica Distilleria Quaglia
2 oz. Rosolio al Bergamotto (bergamot liqueur)
Scant 1 jigger (1 1/3 oz.) mezcal
Ice cubes
Orange peel powder, for garnish
Finely ground cardamom, for garnish

Makes 1 cocktail

Combine plum juice, orange brandy, Rosolio al Bergamotto, and
mezcal in a cocktail shaker. Fill with ice cubes, cover tightly, and
shake until cold, about 30 seconds. Strain into a cocktail glass
and garnish lightly with orange powder and cardamom. Serve
immediately.

FRANCO PEPE
CIRO OLIVA

PIZZAIOLI

FRANCO

PEPE

Franco Pepe is handing out *pizze a libretto* (small pizza dressed with tomato sauce, garlic and oregano, and folded twice, two Euros a pop) to the people who are starting to line up in front of his restaurant. By the time the night is over the line will have stretched all the way to the end of the alley. People don't seem to mind: they know it's worth it.

Italy's best pizzaiolo lives and works here, in Caiazzo, a small town surrounded by antique walls (*mura ciclopiche*, Cyclopean masonry, so called because they're built with massive boulders) in the area known as Sannio, about forty minutes outside of Naples, halfway between the mountains and the sea. He's the best not because I think so, or because of the countless awards he's received, or the constant pilgrimage by colleagues who come from all over the world to meet him. He's the best because of the way he has been able to reconcile tradition and experimentation, both in his product and in his business, revitalizing a marginalized territory and developing a pizza that is quite unlike any other: undoubtedly gourmet in its conception (Pepe prides himself on having absorbed the lesson of many chef friends, transferring it to his pizza) yet traditional at the core; pillow-soft and custardy, with a big edge (the cornicione) and just the right amount of surface crunch; delicious, and supremely digestible. You eat it and you know it's Pepe's.

Take the Margherita Sbagliata, arguably his most celebrated creation (together with the outstanding Calzone con Scarola Riccia, which is an original recipe of his father's), made with mozzarella di bufala and two reductions, one of pomodoro riccio, a local heirloom tomato, and one of basil, which are added only after cooking. It looks like a modernist painting, it tastes like home. And heaven.

At Pepe's it all starts with the dough, about 550 pounds (which will make seven hundred balls of dough) hand-mixed daily by Franco and his team in wooden dough boxes, under the watchful eye of (a photo of) Pope Francis. Five hundred and fifty pounds of dough, hand-mixed: take a moment to let that sink in. "I am not against commercial mixers," he tells me as he stands in front of one of his two ovens, performing a routine temperature check. "I'm interested in technology, and I would like to experiment on the extent to which we can scale back on manual labor without losing that human factor, which is essential to the development of any handmade product's identity."

Today is a good day, but I have been at Pepe's on numerous occasions and I have often seen him plagued by a recurring tendinitis, caused by the strain on his forearm's muscles. Yet he'd never give up hand-mixing: it's as fundamental to the proper development of his dough as the choice of salt (from the salt beds of Trapani, in Sicily), water (which he decants), and flour (the "0 Pepe", a blend he has custom-made and adjusted monthly).

Pepe's pizza has a melt-on-your-tongue quality; it's like exceptional sourdough bread, except lighter. I once had ten tasting-size pies for dinner here: I slept like a baby and woke up with a solid appetite. The secret of this impressive digestibility can be traced back to fermentation, which in this case is achieved through a mix of *pasta di riporto* (a reserved portion of the previous day's dough) and yeast; the dough then rests for twelve hours at twenty-four degrees Celsius. The final mass is looser than the normal dough: it contains seventy percent water, more than the amount prescribed by the official guidelines for traditional Neapolitan pizza.

The art of the Neapolitan pizzaiolo is on Unesco's list of intangible cultural heritages. Pepe, however, doesn't consider himself to be one: he is a different species and he knows it. He's generous and kind, with an ascetic, guru-like aura around him, but this doesn't mean he's not fully aware of his talent and singularity.

He learned the craft from his father, who had learned it from his. Grandpa Pepe had a bakery, which at one point had taken to serving simple dishes and pizza. Franco's father opened a proper pizzeria on Caiazzo's main square and that's where Franco (who originally studied to become a gym teacher) and his brothers started out.

"I remember my dad walking home late at night after closing time. He'd cross the square holding an empty can of San Marzano tomatoes filled with the residual embers from the pizza oven. My brothers and I would stand on our balcony on the other side of the piazza, see the red glowing streak, and know he'd be home soon."

When Franco decided to branch out on his own, it wasn't without friction. He later reconciled with his brothers but for a long time the tale of the two Pepe clans was like a page out of the Montague and Capulets' saga. During the years of his climb to fame (this is the man who organized a private tasting for two Italian presidents, at their own request) his relationship with his wife and children also became frayed. That chapter too is resolved and today Franco works side by side with his son Stefano (he also has a daughter, Francesca).

Pepe in Grani is housed in a restored eighteenth-century three-story palmento (a traditional building dedicated to the pressing of olives or grapes) with two dining rooms, a veranda, a garden, two kitchens, two guest bedrooms, and a small terrace with an arresting view, which can be reserved for more intimate dinners. There is also Authentica, a chef's table where Pepe himself prepares and bakes one pizza at a time

for no more than eight guests, explaining the process as he goes. "I built it to honor the memory of my father, who used to entertain his guests as he was preparing his pizza. I wanted to restore that sense of closeness." Over the years his operation has grown to include not just an ever-expanding menu in Caiazzo, but also a second location, La Filiale, in Franciacorta, inside the luxury wine resort L'Albereta.

Pepe's team goes well beyond the walls of his pizzerie. He works with several nutritionists and with agronomist Vincenzo Coppola for what has become the main focus of his research: finding the elusive point where deliciousness, health, and cultural sustainability meet. Upon request he now makes doughs with two specialty flours, einkorn and Nostrum, a blend of populations of an old variety of Durum wheat, Autonomia, grown from seeds salvaged from local households, where the tradition of home-baking was never really lost. These flours have weaker gluten and therefore require many technical adjustments to be mixed and shaped properly.

Vincenzo Coppola, who is responsible for the successful reintroduction of the Autonomia wheat crops, is also in charge of guiding Pepe in the rediscovery of local ingredients that not only carry incredible nutritional benefits (like the pomodoro riccio of the Margherita Sbagliata, which is very high in antioxidants), but also help revitalize artisanal micro-productions in the Alto Casertano area: chickpeas from the colline caiatine (the hills around Caiazzo), onions from Alife, Lenzariello beans, the pungent conciato romano cheese, and a local breed of black swine (nero casertano). Many of these artisans are in their late twenties and have come to farming by choice and not because of family expectations. They see Pepe as a beacon. I know Pepe too well not to know this puts pressure on him—the pressure of other people's expectations. But this is the life you choose when you're the best.

Sensazioni di Costiera
Costiera Vibes (Fried Pizza with Anchovies and Tomatoes)

Fried pizza is typical of the Italian center and south. In his version, Franco Pepe celebrates the typical flavors and scents of the Costiera (the coast around the Sorrentine peninsula), without giving up his signature feather-light dough.

2 quarts vegetable oil, for frying
6 balls of Pizza Fritta Dough (recipe follows)
1 ½ teaspoon garlic powder
1 ½ teaspoon cayenne pepper, or to taste
1 vine-ripe tomato, sliced
24 Cetara anchovies packed in oil
1 ½ teaspoon finely chopped parsley
1 ½ teaspoon finely grated or julienned lemon zest

For 6 individual-sized pizzas

Heat the oil in a large Dutch oven or wok over medium-high heat. Drop in a tiny piece of dough to test the oil; if it sizzles and floats to the surface immediately, the oil is ready.

Meanwhile, transfer the ball of dough to a floured surface, and stretch it with your fingers into a 6-inch round. With a small, sharp knife, prick 4 to 5 small holes in the center of the dough. Carefully lower it into the hot oil, cook for 15 seconds, then flip. Cook until the bottom is lightly golden, 30 to 45 seconds; flip and cook for another 30 to 45 seconds. The pizza should be golden on both sides, but not overly crisp. Transfer to a paper towel-lined plate to drain for 15 seconds, then to a cutting board. Sprinkle pizza with ¼ teaspoon garlic powder and ¼ teaspoon cayenne pepper, and cut into quarters. Top each wedge with 1 slice of tomato, 1 anchovy, ¼ teaspoon parsley and ¼ teaspoon lemon zest. Roll, prick, and fry remaining balls of dough, one at a time, and top each pizza with remaining ingredients. Serve immediately.

Pizza Fritta Dough
1 cup water, at room temperature
2 teaspoons salt
3 cups (14 oz.) 00 flour or all-purpose flour
3/4 teaspoon active dry yeast

For 6 individual pizzas

Combine water and salt in the bowl of a stand mixer fitted with a dough hook. Mix on low speed until salt dissolves. With the mixer on low speed, begin adding the flour, one tablespoon at a time. After about half of the flour has been incorporated, add the yeast, then gradually add the rest of the flour.

Knead on low speed for 5 to 7 minutes (15 to 20 if kneading by hand), until the dough becomes smooth and elastic. Dough will remain somewhat sticky. Remove the bowl from the stand mixer, cover with a clean dishcloth, and let rise for 4 hours.

Turn the dough out onto a lightly floured surface, cut into 6 equal pieces. Using floured hands, gently shape each piece into a ball by folding the dough under itself. Place balls of dough, seam side down, on a heavily floured surface. Cover with a dampened cloth, and let rise until doubled in size, about 2 hours, before shaping and frying.

CIRO

OLIVA

In the past few years the world has upped its pizza game, and exceptional pies can now be found from Los Angeles to Tokyo. It's an incentive for a new generation of Italian pizzaioli to rethink the entire experience, intensifying their research on the science of dough and ingredients, and designing viable businesses while giving back to their communities.

One thing that hasn't changed is the visceral love surrounding these pizzaioli: more than chefs, they are worshipped with a particular brand of devotion that borders on fanaticism. They are perceived as one with the people, but also as patron saints. Which is why spending a day with Ciro Oliva of Concettina ai Tre Santi walking the streets of his own Rione Sanità, in the grittiest, yet most picturesque (and inexorably gentrifying) part of Naples, is quite the surreal experience.

Ciro, a fourth generation pizzaiolo, is exuberant and speaks a mile a minute, mixing English and Italian. Because doing just one thing would be impossible for this powerhouse (who was married at 19 and has two kids). While he talks, he also walks, gestures, and poses for his in-house photographer. An acquaintance zips by on his Vespa and stops to say hi; Ciro borrows the man's scooter for a quick ride to the end of the street, his immaculate, ankle-long apron flapping.

We go to Palazzo dello Spagnuolo, a triumph of hazelnut and pistachio-colored rococo architecture. I soon realize this is a staged catwalk: the young pizzaiolo leading the way in chef's whites, snapping his fingers and flashing his smile, while the owners of the botteghe and food stalls we pass come out to shake his hand and exchange a few words. Some ask for a picture. Apparently, a crew from *Chef's Table* just finished filming an episode of the new pizza season here. It's all very theatrical. In this neighborhood, where even a kid will tell you Totò, the Charlie Chaplin of Italy, was born and Vittorio De Sica's Academy-Award winning *Yesterday, Today, and Tomorrow*, with Sophia Loren, was filmed, the picturesque has become currency.

"They all want to take a photo of me with a backdrop of the alley and the hanging laundry," says Ciro, but he's interested in more than being a prop. "I want Concettina to be a humble home where people can go find the best of the best, from pizza to the glasses we serve our wine in. That's why I pay my staff well: my dad, who has been working for forty years, never made as much as they make now!"

At Concettina ai Tre Santi, which is named after Ciro's great-grandmother and the nearby street altar, clients can choose to leave a pizza sospesa, literally a "standby pizza": this extra pizza, which they pay for but don't consume, will be served to a person in need (the same custom exists for coffee in many Italian bars). This is only a small example of how Ciro, despite his grandiloquent attitude, his youthful branding scheme (and the bouncer manning the constant line outside Concettina), enjoys staying connected to his 'hood.

He supports a local version of 4-H, "Casa dei Cristallini," where neighborhoods kids can gather after school to study, learn practical skills, and play, away from the streets: every year he helps raise funds to allow them to study English abroad, and at Concettina he uses beautifully hand-painted dishes made in the club's pottery lab. "Esco pazzo per la mise," he says, meaning he's crazy about a good mise en place. It shows.

His menu at Concettina is an ode to the many incarnations of pizza, from the past to the present, and to all those elements of popular "lowly" Neapolitan cuisine that go well with pizza. There's *montanarine* (small fried pizza balls topped with a variety of hearty ingredients); the *rind'o ruot*, a traditional pizza baked in a round dish; a more tame but no less enticing margherita or marinara; the Panino Annarell' with artichokes, provolone cheese, and aged prosciutto crudo (page 195); calzone filled with ricotta, a traditional pork ragù, and aged Parmigiano-Reggiano; a frisella (a sort of crunchy half-bagel) with lentils, hazelnuts, rosemary, and lemon thyme; fried pizza filled with smoked amberjack, ricotta, dried seaweed, and orange zest; Ciro's version of Neapolitan zuppa forte (or soffritto), made with the best parts of black Casertano pork and sausage, slow braised, and served in a mini copper pot, with stale bread to dip. Some of the dishes trace back to his family, others to Massimo Bottura, whom he cites as an inspiration and friend. But he's quick to point out, "A chef can teach you a technique, but we pizzaioli come up with the concepts. I don't want to learn someone else's idea, I want to stick with mine, and work with things you can only find here." One can order a colorfully presented twelve-course tasting menu based around pizza. Though this is something more and more pizzaioli are offering, Ciro goes the extra mile. All this is backed by a small but well-stocked cellar, with a truly enjoyable selection of Champagne.

As we get ready to leave I'm trying to make sense of all this: the LED-powered "Sanità" signs, the paintings of Pulcinella (an historic Neapolitan mask) by artist Lello Esposito, the vases shaped like heads of Totò and other local legends made by Marco Ferrigno, one of the city's great artisans specializing in handcrafting Nativity scenes. How much of it is cliché? How much is smart set design?

"I'll tell you what my objective is," says Ciro, with a Colgate-perfect smile: "Tradition that feels simple, sophisticated, and playful, at the same time." He waves goodbye, as children play soccer around him. And. . . scene.

Panino Annarell'
Panino Annarell'

This panino is a small, round version of the saltimbocca napoletano, a traditional flat sub made with pizza dough. Ciro named it his after his Mom, who used to prepare it for his merenda (snack) and serves it with artichokes in three different textures.

2 lemons
8 artichokes
Extra virgin olive oil
Salt
Pepper
3/4 teaspoon freshly squeezed lemon juice, or more to taste
½ teaspoon freshly grated lemon zest
4 cups canola oil
3 oz. Taleggio cheese (you may substitute brie), cut into small cubes
4 Ciro's pizza dough balls, proofed (recipe follows)
Semolina flour, for dusting
2 oz. thinly sliced prosciutto crudo

Makes 4 small sandwiches

Fill a large bowl with water; squeeze the juice of 2 lemons into it. With a sharp paring knife, trim away the tough outer leaves of the artichoke to expose the tender inner leaves and heart. Trim the outer layer of the stem. Cut in half through the core, remove furry choke, if present, and place artichoke hearts immediately in the bowl of lemon water. Add a teaspoon of salt and let rest for 2 hours. Rinse artichoke hearts; set aside 3 halves for frying.

Bring a medium saucepan full of water to a boil over high heat. When boiling, add 2 tablespoons of salt and the remaining artichoke hearts. Boil until tender when poked with a fork, 12 to 15 minutes. Drain until cool enough to handle. Transfer 4 halves to a cutting board and cut into thin wedges; remove any outer leaves that remain too tough to chew. Place wedges in a bowl, dress with olive oil, ¼ teaspoon lemon juice, ½ teaspoon lemon zest, and salt and pepper to taste; set aside. Combine the remaining boiled artichokes in a blender or food processor with ½ cup olive oil, ½ teaspoon lemon juice, and ground black pepper. Blend until smooth. Taste for salt and acidity; adjust seasonings accordingly. If the cream still contains tough fibers after blending, you may filter it through a fine mesh sieve. Set aside artichoke cream.

Heat 4 cups of canola oil in a medium saucepan over high heat. Slice 3 remaining, raw artichoke heart halves into thin spears, removing any outer leaves that remain too tough to chew. When oil is hot enough that a crumb of bread sizzles immediately upon contact, carefully add the artichokes and fry until golden and crisp, 7 to 10 minutes. Remove from oil with a slotted spoon or spider and drain on a paper towel-lined plate; sprinkle with salt.

Place a pizza stone (or baking sheet lined with parchment paper) in cold oven and preheat to 500°F. When oven is hot, sprinkle semolina flour over pizza stone or baking sheet. Using a floured spatula or a pizza paddle, transfer dough balls to the hot baking stone (or baking sheet). Close oven immediately and cook, undisturbed for 4 minutes. Remove rolls from oven and immediately slice in half with kitchen shears or heavy-duty scissors. Spread a layer of artichoke cream inside each roll, and divide the cheese among them. Close the rolls, return to oven and bake for another 2 minutes, or until cheese is melted. Remove from oven, reopen the sandwiches and stuff each with artichoke spears, fried artichokes chips, and slices of prosciutto crudo. Serve warm, with extra virgin olive oil and sea salt, for dipping.

Ciro's Dough
3 cups all-purpose flour
2 teaspoons salt
Scant ½ teaspoon active dry yeast
1 ¼ cup water, room temperature
Extra virgin olive oil
Semolina flour, for dusting

Makes 18 small pizza dough balls

Place water in a bowl and sprinkle the yeast over the surface; set aside in a warm place for 5 minutes.

Grease a large bowl with olive oil. Combine flour and salt in the bowl of a stand mixer fitted with a dough hook. With the mixer running on low speed, gradually add the yeast and the water. Knead on low speed until the dough becomes smooth and elastic, 5 to 7 minutes (10 to 15 if kneading by hand). Dough will remain somewhat sticky. Transfer dough to greased bowl, cover with a clean dishcloth, and let rise at room temperature for 8 hours.

Turn the dough out onto a lightly floured surface, cut into 18 equal pieces. Using floured hands, gently shape each piece into a ball, by pulling gently and folding the dough under itself. Line 2 baking sheets with parchment and lightly dust the paper with semolina flour. Place balls of dough on prepared baking sheets, with the seam of each ball on the bottom. Cover with a dampened cloth, and let rise at room temperature for 4 hours, or until doubled in size.

DIEGO ROSSI
FRANCESCO CAPUZZO DOLCETTA
LORENZO COSTA
PIETRO VERGANO
ANDREA GHERRA
STEFANO & MATTIA MANIAS
THE FOODERS
MARTINA MICCIONE
CARLA DE GIROLAMO

FORCES OF NEO-OSTERIE & NEO-TRATTORIE

198

DIEGO

ROSSI

He has a signet ring engraved with a very peculiar subject: tripe. Not your regular crest, but then again Diego Rossi has *trippa* on his mind almost 24/7. He loves offal, with a visceral (pun intended), all consuming, borderline obsessive love.

"I find it so much more interesting than regular cuts of meat," says the young Veronese, smiling under his signature mustache, while tying up a makeshift bandana, fashioned out of a kitchen towel, around his head, his tattooed, sinewy biceps flexing (he's a gym rat). "Meat is meat; there's only a certain range of flavor nuances you can extract from it, whereas internal organs have very specific textures and flavors, and they all require knowledge and practice to cook well."

Trippa is also the name of the Milanese restaurant Diego opened with partner Pietro Caroli in 2015. It was the year of Expo Milano, the food-themed world exposition ("Feeding the planet, energy for life" was the official tagline) that forever changed the face of the city, igniting a renaissance that turned a productive yet slightly boring metropolis into a vibrant destination—starting with its restaurant scene.

Trippa quickly became a case study: it is still Milan's hottest table, the hardest place to get in. Diego and Pietro hit a home run by filling a niche, introducing a format that was obviously though shockingly still missing, and not so easy to nail: the neo-trattoria.

Experience is what really makes a trattoria "trattoria." Food is not secondary—it has to be good, fresh, prepared with sound technique yet not overly conceptualized—but a trattoria is first and foremost a feeling: the uncomplicated nourishment of the body and the soul. It is assisted entertainment, at a reasonable price. If a fine dining restaurant is essentially chef's territory and an osteria is traditionally a host's domain, a trattoria should be a plot of land shared equally by the kitchen and the floor. Diego and his crew know this well.

Diego's background is in fine dining: he worked under Norbert Niederkofler at Restaurant St. Hubertus, in the Dolomites, and with Juri Chiotti (page 56) at Antiche Contrade in Piedmont. "It wasn't easy to let go of that background. The first week at Trippa I lost eight pounds. I was stressing out because I kept thinking 'I can make this better, I can do something more to it, I can make it perfect!'" He felt he was compromising too much, that the things he was making were too simple. "It wasn't fine dining, but it wasn't simple either. Now I realize so many high-profile chefs feel the same way, not understanding the historic moment we're living in. It's too bad, because they'd be so much stronger if they took one step back. If they did, there'd be fifty great neo-trattorie, not just a handful."

When people ask Diego what kind of cuisine his makes, his answer is "Cucina d'improvvisazione, ma non improvvisata"—cuisine that is ad-libbed, but not improvised. Another common question is "What's your specialty?" His response is that he doesn't have one; a good chef has to be able to do everything. In Diego's case this also means not being tied to one specific region: his is not Milanese cuisine (though there are elements of local tradition); his inspiration comes from all over the peninsula. His profound knowledge of products, supported by a network of suppliers few other Milan restaurants can rival, is what allows him to make simple dishes that are as satisfying as they are fully formed. He's not just throwing a couple good ingredients together and calling it cucina. "I study, I'm curious, when I'm into something, I want to learn everything there is to know about it. I can talk a butcher's ear off for hours." This is an approach that is as empowering as it is limiting.

It's empowering because few other chefs can confidently break down a whole sheep and use every single part of it (I watched him do just that in 30 minutes flat in front of an audience of a few hundred), glance at a cut of beef and gauge the best cooking time according to how much fat it has (almost all meat at Trippa is cooked à la minute), or come up with a bunch of the day's specials at a moment's notice. And he doesn't just stop at meat. He makes a brilliant vegetarian version of classic beef carpaccio, with extra thin slices of watermelon, Lodigiano cheese, arugula, and candied lemon, and every summer he stocks up on long, sinuous, and sweet Trombetta zucchini, found only on the French and west Ligurian Riviera, which he serves with apricot jam and a caciocavallo podolico cheese fondue. And then there are his fish: "Yesterday I got a thirty-pound amberjack and I cooked not just the filets, but also the swim bladder, heart, tripe, liver and milt. Then I sold the head. Actually, I believe I'm better with fish than with meat."

Trippa is open for dinner only. This means an eight-hour shift: not bad for an industry known to crush its professionals under a massive workload. "We can't plan ahead too much, otherwise we'd spend too much time prepping. So we have a few signature dishes that are always on the menu," —like fried tripe (page 205), tripe with tomato sauce, grilled bone marrow and veal with tuna-caper sauce—"and each day I come up with a few specials, about 10 servings each." Obviously, these specials will never be as finessed as the signature dishes are. But he'll take a certain degree of imperfection in exchange for freedom. Menus that are set in stone, he says, hold the client hostage, and they're not fun enough for the chef. You can see why this approach is also a limiting one: in a way, it leads to a one-man show.

Diego Rossi, like Damiano Donati (page 82), doesn't write down any recipe. Sitting at the kitchen-facing counter at Trippa one will typically see him do a lot of actual cooking and, once the service has started, man the pass and frequently call out to his number two, to make sure he's written down some procedure they've just come up with. "I personally don't need recipes: once you know an ingredient, you know what to do with it. Not to sound like an egomaniac, but didn't Mozart compose music in his head?"

This is like saying you can make Diego Rossi's cuisine only if you're Diego Rossi, and that there can be no Trippa without him. Several investors have approached him, dangling the carrot of a Hong Kong or New York location. The prestige would be enormous. And yet: "I don't see how I could open them without being there in person all the time: I couldn't be a consultant, it wouldn't work." There's no manual one can buy to learn what he does, no way of really guessing sheep's tartare will go well with grated pecorino cheese, or that a horse skirt steak will pair nicely with a pear compote, or how to serve rooster's testicles or chicken's gizzards. One has to painstakingly learn about the product and have the same sort of spark (and spunk) he has, paired with an extraordinary drive—and a keen sense for atmosphere.

"I kept going out to eat and I couldn't find the kind of place I needed." So he built it. "A place where people can relax, be rowdy if they want, and eat some kickass food, which I happen to know everything about. So if you want to learn more about it, I can explain it to you. Or a waiter will."

The front of house is equally responsible for creating Trippa's atmosphere as the kitchen is. Pietro Caroli manages it with the lightest touch, sly and firm, and his staff is funny in a sometimes caustic way.

The ochre-colored walls are covered with vintage pictures: the actual families of Trippa's staff. There's a rotary phone, guitars, tilted bistro-style mirrors, old radios and Fender amps, even a foosball table (downstairs, next to the cellar and the staff's changing rooms). "The most crucial thing when opening a restaurant is not what you have in mind; rather, it's what the client's perception of what the place is. The same goes for what's in the dish. Maybe you think what you're doing is simple but then it starts feeling a bit too elaborate; maybe you think you built a warm, informal place, but it turns out people don't see it as such. I think when you walk into Trippa you can't help but thinking "this is a trattoria." A trattoria can be contemporary, but it has to feel convivial. It also has to feel Italian."

The philological element of names is also important: a trattoria is not an osteria, and if you name a place "osteria" without respecting its canon then, to quote Diego, "you're fucking with Italy." It shouldn't come as a surprise that an osteria is in fact what he's planning to open next. He shows me a note on his iPhone: color schemes, interiors, menu ideas. There will be a whole mortadella and a whole porchetta, sliced to order, sitting on the counter; jars of pickles and vegetables packed in oil; vermouth, grappe, and natural wines; great bread, cold pasta with beans and pork rinds; a big counter and thick, basic plates, the unbreakable kind. ("They're all using these Nordic-looking ones and I get it, they make any dish look amazing, but that's not me.")

The menu is, fittingly, still in flux, but one thing he's sure of: he'll serve a bull's tartare. "Because I like to experiment with unusual meats, particularly if I've never worked with them before. Did I tell you about that time I cooked a bear's foot?"

Trippa Fritta
Fried Tripe

Although Diego Rossi is originally from Verona, his cooking references multiple regional cuisines. Case in point is his Trippa Frita, a dish that is originally from Liguria. For his version, Rossi uses honeycomb tripe—the second stomach and the most coveted of the four stomachs of the cow—because it allows him to obtain a double texture; crunchy on the outside and chewy on the inside. He finishes it with rosemary and pepper because they remind him of his favorite potato chips. Tripe must be cleaned and partially cooked before being sold, and it has often been bleached. Look for unbleached tripe if possible, which will be a yellowish-beige color, and avoid the bright-white tripe that betrays the use of harsh chemicals.

1 ½ lbs. honeycomb tripe
1 ½ cups all-purpose flour
5 cups peanut oil, for frying
Salt and pepper
2 sprigs of rosemary

Serves 4

Place the tripe in a large stockpot and cover with cold water. Bring to a boil over medium-high heat, then reduce heat to low and simmer until tripe is tender, 2 to 3 hours. You should be able to poke a hole in the tripe with your finger when it's ready. Drain the tripe, and when it's cool enough to handle, cut into strips about 1/3-inch-wide and 2 ½ inches long.

Combine the flour and tripe in a large, wide bowl; toss until the strips are completely coated.

Heat the oil in a large Dutch oven or wok to 350°F, or until the oil sputters when you toss in a pinch of flour. Fry the tripe, in batches, until golden brown and crisp, 5 to 6 minutes. Using a spider or slotted spoon, transfer the fried tripe onto a paper towel-lined dish to drain briefly. Season tripe with salt and pepper to taste, and sprinkle with rosemary leaves. Serve immediately.

FRANCESCO
CAPUZZO DOLCETTA

Have you ever seen a pullet's insides? Have you ever seen a cluster of eggs that have to yet develop their shell? Or the contents of a gizzard?

"Look at it, check for yourself how fresh it still smells," urges Francesco Capuzzo Dolcetta , executive chef of Marzapane, in Rome, as he hands me the gizzard he has just sliced open, with its contents of vegetable mush, undigested seeds, carrot bits, corn fragments—yes, fresh smelling.

"In some countries, they'd cook and serve it," he points out as he keeps disassembling the pullet's carcass with his skillful, unrushed knifework, neatly organizing cuts of meat and organs on his station as he goes. He shows me the pullet's "oysters," two oval, smooth pieces of dark meat positioned near the thigh, in what could be considered the small of the bird's back. He carefully skewers them, glazes them, and then starts grilling them over a kamado, a traditional Japanese barbecue.

A few minutes later he'll sear the heart of a free-range black swine from the Nebrodi on a Big Green Egg, then he'll fire some more skewers on the kamado (chicken and peppers, pork meatballs and prickly pear, mackerel, chanterelles) and start work on a few of his signature dishes: the mallard leg en croûte, the capellini pasta with beef butter and licorice (recipe on page 213), a whole barbecued fish with fermented apple sauce. The pullet will be served with mussels and lemon leaves.

And to think that when he first sent out his resume, not one Roman restaurant got back to him. Fortunately, Francesco Capuzzo Dolcetta is not one to give up (he is gracious, almost chivalrous, but quick to put his foot down if something he believes in is questioned).

While the brigade, four people in total, breaks for the staff meal (freshly made tagliatelle with barely-seared cherry tomatoes and shiso), Mario Sansone, owner and host of Marzapane, moves behind the counter at the entrance, making sure knives are sharp, and that all charcuterie and cheese are well stocked in the brand new refrigerated cases. Alberto and I sit on the stools in front of him and have a snack of falafel, pastrami, pickles, and vegetables preserved in oil with warm bread—all house-made. We try a red pepper "ketchup" I could eat by the spoonful until my arteries exploded. I look around, consider the light streaming in, the grays and beiges and the wood, glance at the guys quietly working behind the panoramic kitchen window, and think I could see myself eating here a few times a week, probably never having the same experience twice. Boy, has this restaurant changed in just a matter of months.

Earlier that morning we were at the Testaccio market with Francesco, shopping for groceries. He knew all the vendors. "I was born in Florence, and grew up nearby," he explains. "My mother Daniela opened one of the first cooking schools for foreigners not far from here. She'd start her classes at the slaughterhouse, over there, where the School of Architecture is now.

He gets groceries and sheep's milk for gelato from the market here or at the Campagna Amica farmers' market at Circo Massimo. Meat comes from a dream team of suppliers: Agostino, the "father" of the Slow Food Presidium black swine of the Nebrodi, Zilieri for fowl and boar, Cazzamali for kidneys, Liberati for everything else.

Francesco loves the hunt for the perfect, freshest ingredient, an obsession he shares with Mario (they came up with the concept for the "new" Marzapane together.) Francesco gets it from growing up in a family of recreational foragers and spearfishermen and from his professional nomadism: after Alma he interned at Caino, a Tuscan restaurant (sadly deemed uncool by most young gastronomic cliques) where generations of exceptional chefs have learned to choose and respect ingredients, absorbing the priceless guidance and fierce motherly love of Valeria Piccini. After Caino, he moved to France: he worked with Marco Viganò, the Troisgros (for more than a year), finally with Mathieu Rostaing-Tayard at the now defunct and very much missed Café Sillon, in Lyon. Then came a transformative month spent between Tokyo and Osaka.

"People think the best lesson you can learn in France is technique," observes Francesco, whose culinary foundations are indeed rock solid (and whose love for pâté en croûte and terrines knows no boundaries). "But for me that only accounts for a small percentage: what I was taught was a very specific approach to the work. Order, sacrifice, consistency in research. Mathieu was a maniac of precision even if there were only three people in the kitchen and not forty, as in a grand maison. From the bistro experience with him I also learned something else: the power of imagination."

A love for bistronomie was also the engine behind Mario's decision to shake things up at Marzapane where, prior to Francesco's promotion from sous chef to executive in 2019, Spanish chef Alba Esteve Ruiz had been in charge of the kitchen. Initially, when Mario left his job as sales director of Eataly to open a restaurant, his references were Septime and Le Chateaubriand, in Paris, and most importantly Giovanni Passerini, a long-time friend and source of inspiration. "I started with the idea of something easy and well done, but it soon morphed into something else: we went from jeans to suits, from telling our customers the story of our tomatoes to ordering from catalogues. Our goal was a Michelin star. But the higher we set the bar the more impersonal everything became."

Hitting reset was the only possible option. This meant two things: parting ways, amicably, with Alba and rethinking the way people could interact with the restaurant. A light renovation has made room for two counters, one at the entrance, with its display of gastronomia selections, one with a view of the kitchen. This, together with a smart recalibration of the cuisine, allows clients to choose what kind of experience they want to have.

It's two restaurants in one: the first more informal and quick (lunch or aperitivo with day's specials, fritti, yakitori-style skewers, delicious salumi and cheeses, sott'oli and sott'aceti, vegetables preserved in oil or vinegar, the second more substantial (dinner with free-hand tasting menus). Both equally fun. Even the most elaborate dishes here are extremely direct, based on "a wise handling of the best ingredients," as Francesco says, where "wise" stands for a natural, sometimes even "primal" path to transformation, such as the one provided by the two barbecues, or by slow maceration. Now, more than ever, a chef's priority is to serve something good that their guests can understand: "If they don't recognize what's in the dish, then we have failed."

Capellino con Burro di Manzo e Liquirizia
Capellini Pasta with "Beef Butter" and Licorice

Francesco Dolcetta Capuzzo's idea to repurpose the thick fat covering beef kidneys (suet), after smoking, melting, filtering, and re-solidifying it, came from a desire to use every part of the animal. The result proved to be an intriguing substitute to butter, boasting a unique smooth, velvety texture, and a sumptuous aroma perfectly complemented by a balsamic licorice powder, made by grinding hard candies of pure, unsweetened licorice (such as Amarelli Spezzatina, which can be found in Italian specialty shops or ordered online) that are common in Italy. The resulting sauce is quite rich, so the serving sizes in this recipe are relatively small. (Note: Roma rice has distinctive, large, rounded grains which are ideal for this recipe—see page 18 for more info. If you can't find Roma, Carnaroli or Arborio will do in a pinch.)

3.5 oz. high-quality beef suet
½ cup Roma rice
10 oz. capellini pasta
1 tablespoon black licorice (see headnote)
1 teaspoon Sriracha (recipe follows)
1 teaspoon lemon juice, or more to taste

Special equipment:
Smoker, such as a pellet or offset smoker; or a charcoal grill

Serves 4

Prepare smoker and heat to 170°F. Add the suet and smoke until golden brown and fragrant, 30 to 40 minutes. If using a charcoal grill, position about 15 hot coals onto one side of the charcoal tray and place a disposable aluminum pan full of water on the other side of the tray. Scatter soaked wood chips over the coals and place the suet on the grill, directly over the pan of water. Close the lid and smoke for 30 to 40 minutes, adjusting the air vents to maintain a temperature of about 170°F.

Remove suet from smoker and cut into small cubes. Place in a medium-sized saucepan over low heat and cook, stirring often, until fat melts completely, about 30 minutes. Filter through a fine mesh sieve, discard solids and reserve liquid.

Place the rice in a small saucepan and cover with 1 inch of cold water. Bring to a boil then simmer, uncovered, until rice is very well cooked and has absorbed all the water. Let cool slightly, then transfer to a blender or food processor and blend until smooth, adding up to a tablespoon of water if necessary to obtain a smooth cream. Filter rice cream through a fine mesh sieve and set aside.

Grind the licorice into a fine powder with a mortar and pestle or spice grinder, set aside.

Place a large pot of water over high heat; when water boils add 2 tablespoons salt. Meanwhile, combine the melted suet, 2 tablespoons of rice cream, 1 teaspoon homemade Sriracha (or less,

to taste) and 2 tablespoons water in a large nonstick frying pan or wok over medium-low heat.

Cook the pasta in the boiling water until just al dente. Drain, reserving some of the cooking water; add pasta to the sauce and turn heat up to high. Shake the pan to combine pasta with sauce; add more cooking water as needed to coat the pasta and create a smooth sauce. Remove from heat, add lemon juice to taste. Divide pasta between warm plates and sprinkle with licorice powder. Serve immediately.

Homemade Sriracha
20 cloves garlic, peeled and sliced
¾ lb. whole fresh spicy chili peppers (about 3 cups, seeded and finely chopped)
½ cup white wine vinegar
2/3 cup honey

Makes about ¼ cup

Place the sliced garlic in a small saucepan and cover with cold water. Bring to a boil, then strain garlic and return to the pot. Cover with cold water and repeat; do this a total of three times. Drain garlic.

Combine blanched garlic, diced chili peppers, vinegar, honey, and 2 tablespoons water in a small or medium saucepan over medium-low heat. Cook, stirring occasionally, until completely soft, about 40 minutes. You may add more water, one tablespoon at a time, if all the liquid evaporates before the cooking is finished. Remove from heat and let cool slightly. Purée in a food processor or blender until smooth, adding another tablespoon of water if necessary. Filter through a fine mesh sieve, pressing with a rubber spatula to release all the liquid; discard solids. Place in a clean saucepan over low heat. Cook, stirring often, until mixture has reduced to a thick paste, about 10 minutes. Remove from heat, transfer to a small jar and refrigerate until ready to use.

Razza, Lardo e Foglie di Fico Sotto Aceto
Stingray, Lardo, and Pickled Fig Leaves

This dish showcases chef Capuzzo's love for light fermentations and pickling, which he mastered while working at renowned Café Sillon in Lyon with chef Mathieu Rostaing-Tayard. The stingray's particular texture is perfectly complemented by the melt-on-your-tongue lardo (cured, aged pork fat). Note the small serving size; it is served as an antipasto and should be considered as such.

2 teaspoons sea salt, plus more for seasoning
2 teaspoons sugar
½ lb. skinless stingray wing
1 ½ oz. lardo very thinly sliced
8 marinated fig leaves (recipe follows)
Extra virgin olive oil
Fig leaf oil, for serving (recipe follows)

Special Equipment:
Candy Thermometer or Frying Thermometer

Serves 2 to 4

Stir together sea salt and sugar in a small bowl or container. Sprinkle generously on both sides of stingray wings. Set aside to cure for 10 minutes. Rinse under running water, pat dry.

Meanwhile, preheat a grill pan or gas grill over high heat. Brush stingray generously with olive oil and cook on hot grill without turning, until the surface of meat is lightly charred 2 to 4 minutes; flip and cook until second side is lightly charred but the inside is still moist, 2 to 4 more minutes.

Place a piece of grilled stingray in the middle of a serving plate. Top with sliced lardo, marinated fig leaves, and a few drops of fig leaf oil. Serve immediately.

Marinated Fig Leaves
2 cups water
¼ cup sugar
1 tablespoon apple cider vinegar
8 young fig leaves, rinsed

Combine water, sugar, and vinegar in a small saucepan over medium heat. Cook, stirring constantly, until water boils and sugar has dissolved. Add fig leaves and remove saucepan from heat. Transfer fig leaves and liquid to a small metal or glass container, making sure that leaves are submerged. Cover tightly and refrigerate for at least 1 month. Strain leaves and pat dry before serving.

Fig Leaf Oil
1 cup grapeseed oil
3.5 oz. fresh fig leaves (appox. 3 medium or 2 large), washed and patted dry

Combine the oil and the fig leaves in a small saucepan and warm over medium heat to 195°F. Carefully transfer hot oil and leaves to a blender and blend until smooth. Pour into a heat-resistant container and let cool to room temperature. Chill in the refrigerator overnight or up to 3 weeks. Filter the oil through a fine mesh sieve before serving.

STEFANO & MATTIA

MANIAS

When in San Sebastian or Bilbao, you do the pintxo crawl. When in Venice, you do the cicchetti crawl. Served at traditional vinerie called "bacari," cicchetti, just like pintxos, are small bites, varied and plentiful, ranging from anything like frittata, salumi, meatballs, cured fish, tartines, to more elaborate renditions of the genre. They are usually served throughout the day, providing vital sustenance for the aperitivo crowd. In a quiet town about an hour from Venice, on the river Tagliamento, two brothers with a background in fine dining are rewriting the cicchetti format in a restaurant that combines the feeling of a rustic country inn with high-end techniques and references.

Stefano and Mattia Manias started working in their family's restaurant as soon as they were big enough to carry a few plates. Their father, Enzo, served barbecued ribs, sausage, and polenta to a not-very-discerning local crowd. Their mother Rosellina worked the front of house. The brothers went to hotel and catering school, and it was assumed that they'd go back to help with the family restaurant. But they took a detour. At fifteen, Stefano received an internship at L'Albereta, in Franciacorta, under maestro Gualtiero Marchesi, who was assisted by one of his most brilliant alumni, Andrea Berton. "It was brutal. The kitchen was thirteen hundred square feet, with a brigade of thirty-six people. We worked sixteen or eighteen hours a day. It was very regimented: every day we'd get in line at the beginning of service to return our dirty aprons and dish cloths and pick up fresh ones, and again at the end of service to take off our toques. Berton would come in to inspect our fridges, and only if everything was in order would we be dismissed for the night."

After Albereta, Stefano went to work at Montecchia, under Massimiliano Alajmo, and then with multi-starred chefs Mauro Uliassi and Enrico Bartolini. Mattia followed a few years later: he ended staying with Alajmos for seven years, at Le Calandre and as part of the initial team at Ristorante Quadri, in Venice, where he met Elena, his future wife. "While we were cutting our teeth in fine dining, our father was our number one fan," says Mattia. "You could tell he missed us, but also that he was inspired by the path we were exploring, and he'd ask us for tips on how to improve his culinary skills. We got him his first roner, and he started using sous-vide."

Eventually the brothers came home and took over the family business, with Elena, who is the pastry chef at Al Cjasal. The idea they wanted to explore was simple: taking something very typical and distinctive (cicchetti) and infusing it with the knowledge they had absorbed during their formative years. They started out with a menu written on an Excel spreadsheet, with a list of dishes, each offered in three different sizes: regular, half-serving, and cicchetto, or small bite. "We wanted people to come here to 'eat an idea.' We concern ourselves with what's beautiful and tastes good," says Stefano. "Now we only serve about ten 'regular' size dishes a week. Our clients prefer a whole meal of cicchetti, basically a tasting menu: they let us choose for them, because we know how to organize the sequence of bites, so there's a crescendo of flavors."

At Al Cjasal you might start with l'Orto, a cold tomato puree topped with a selection of fresh greens from the restaurant's vegetable garden, and continue with a barbecued oyster, cooked à la minute in the open fireplace and topped with a cucumber granita; a soft taco with fried schie (local baby shrimp), raw cuttlefish, and string beans; frog ragù with crispy rice, and squid ink sauce, fava bean and snow pea puree; a cold spaghettino, served with a tropical fruit juice and Adriatic fish; or roast cuttlefish and prawns with almond cream, curry, turmeric, tangerine, and black rice chips. (Seafood, particularly shellfish, mostly caught in nearby Caorle, is a strong feature on the menu, as are vegetables from Al Cjasal's garden, a big square field wedged between two solid walls of corn and two rows of young fruit trees—pomegranates, figs, apricots, plums, apples and sour cherries—not far from the restaurant.) There is also the "Quaglainbleu," a Cordon Bleu-style quail, stuffed with cheese and prosciutto crudo and then fried. The house's signature dish is the Cannolo Veneziano (page 221), a fun take on the Sicilian cannolo, filled with *baccalà mantecato*, a Venetian specialty of creamed dried cod, and finished with marinated red onion. (*Baccalà* is salt cod, but *baccalà mantecato* is made with dried cod or stockfish—a tricky choice of wording unknown to many Italians.)

With an average of fifty customers per service, they need all the help they can get—which is where the previous generation comes in handy. Enzo and Rosellina are still at the restaurant, welcoming guests, overseeing the front of house. "I could tell Dad missed his hosting duties, so we asked him to stay on," says Stefano. Enzo gladly obliged. On any given night, you can see him uncorking bottles from his collection and talking at leisure not just about his constant search for small wine producers, but also about how far Al Cjasal has come. "A few restaurants in the area have taken to serving gourmet versions of cicchetti: they're copying us, and this is good news," Enzo says with a proud smile.

220

Cannolo Veneziano
Savory Venetian Cannolo

A fun take on a Sicilian specialty, with a very Venetian (and savory!) filling, this cannolo has become so popular the Manias brothers have decided to never take it off the menu. Perfect as an antipasto or to accompany aperitivo, it relies on exceptional quality dried cod, also known as stockfish: the brothers have theirs tenderized at Molino Zoratto, a local artisanal mill which is the only facility in Italy specializing in dried cod "beating" (battitura).

½ lb. dried cod (aka stockfish)
1 ¼ cups grapeseed oil, divided
½ of a medium-sized beet, scrubbed and peeled
4 ½ cups white wine vinegar, divided
1 ½ cups sugar
3 red onions, peeled and thinly sliced
10 cannolo shells (recipe follows)

Special Equipment:
Mandoline
Sous vide machine and bags, optional
Candy Thermometer or Frying Thermometer
Pastry bag, optional

Makes 10 cannoli

Rehydrate the salt cod: Cut the dried fish into big pieces and place in a large glass or ceramic bowl. Cover generously with cold water, seal with plastic wrap and refrigerate overnight. The next day, begin replacing the water every 6 to 8 hours; continue this for 3 days.

After second day, thinly slice the beet with a mandoline. Arrange in a single layer in a wide, shallow bowl and cover with ½ cup of white wine vinegar. Cover with plastic wrap and refrigerate overnight. Drain and pat dry the beets, and slice them into thin strips; return to refrigerator until cod is ready.

When the salt cod is rehydrated, drain and insert it into a sous vide bag or a standard zipper-top plastic bag. Add ½ cup water and 1 tablespoon of grapeseed oil; seal bag. Place bag in a sous vide machine, or large pot of hot water and cook at 195°F for 4 hours. (If using a pot of water, check temperature often and do not let it come to a boil.)

Meanwhile, prepare the onions: combine 4 cups of vinegar and the sugar in a medium saucepan over medium-high heat. Stir until the sugar dissolves completely, then add the onions. Bring to a boil, then remove immediately from heat. Let sit for 30 seconds. Strain the onions (save the vinegar-sugar mixture to repeat this process with other vegetables if desired) and set aside.

Carefully pull the bag out of hot water and remove fish from bag, reserving ½ cup of liquid from the bag. Transfer fish to a cutting board and trim carefully, removing skin and bones. Place in the bowl of a stand mixer fitted with the paddle attachment. Add ¼ cup reserved cooking water and beat at low speed for 2 minutes; gradually increase to high speed. After about 5 minutes, reduce to medium speed and add 1 cup of grapeseed oil in a slow, steady stream. Return to high speed and beat for another 10 to 15 minutes, until fluffy and creamy. Add more oil or cooking water as necessary to obtain the desired consistency.

Transfer the fish mixture to a pastry bag (or large zipper-topped plastic bag with a corner cut out). Carefully pipe into each cannolo shell until full. Press some marinated onion and beet strips onto each end of the cannolo. Refrigerate until ready to serve.

Cannolo Shells
If you don't have professional, metal cannoli tubes, you can improvise with heavy-duty aluminum foil: Crumple aluminum foil into 1-inch balls and arrange them into a 6-inch long line. Press them together to make a cylinder and wrap with additional aluminum foil to create a smooth, uniform shape.

1/2 cup plus 2 tablespoons all-purpose flour
2 teaspoons extra virgin olive oil
2 tablespoons Marsala wine
1 teaspoon white wine vinegar
1 teaspoon fresh lemon juice
1 teaspoon sugar
½ teaspoon salt
4-5 cups canola oil, for frying

Special equipment:
Stand Mixer
Cannoli tubes, optional
4-inch round cookie cutter

Combine flour, olive oil, Marsala, vinegar, lemon juice, sugar, and salt in the bowl of a stand mixer fitted with the paddle attachment. Beat on medium-low speed for 5 minutes, then increase to medium-high speed and continue to beat for another 5 to 10 minutes, until the dough is smooth and elastic. Remove dough from bowl and wrap tightly in plastic wrap; refrigerate for at least 30 minutes or overnight.

Cut the dough into pieces and, working one portion at a time, roll them out as thinly as possible (use a pasta machine if you have one). Cut the sheets into 4-inch rounds and wrap each square around a cannoli tube, using a drop of water to wet the dough where it overlaps; press to adhere.

Preheat oven to 150°F. Heat canola oil in a Dutch oven or wok until it reaches 350°F (or until a cube of bread sizzles immediately when dropped into the hot oil). Fry the cannoli (with their metal tubes), one or two at a time, until golden brown, 45 to 60 seconds. Transfer to a paper towel-lined plate and immediately remove the tube, being careful not to break the shell. Repeat with remaining cannoli. Carefully transfer fried cannoli to a parchment-lined cookie sheet and place in preheated oven for 1 ½ hours. Remove from oven and set aside to cool until ready to use.

LORENZO COSTA

& DANIELE BENDANTI

Among the young men and women of the new cucina italiana movement, I've noticed a few commonalities, such as a subversive, ironic streak that is also combined with a wink (or a smirk) that acknowledges they are getting cues from outside the boot. Perhaps the most overt expression of this is a cap that sits on a shelf in dining room of Oltre embroidered with the restaurant's slogan: "MAKE BOLOGNA GREAT AGAIN."

Bologna is a good case study in gastronomic counterculture: a quiet university town and a stronghold of the Italian Left, steeped in a version of tradition so self-referential the most pressing question for first-timers seems to be "where can I find the best tortellini in brodo?" At Oltre, the restaurant owned by Lorenzo Costa and chef Daniele Bendanti, tradition is revisited in the key of cool.

From the street, Oltre looks more like a club than a restaurant. Hundreds of stickers, from Vans to Jesus Jeans to Supreme, cover every inch of the black door. To enter, you have to ring a buzzer. It's a statement. Inside, a massive photo of Michael Jordan stares at customers from one wall. Skateboards and surfboards abound. Menus are illustrated with comic-strip scenes from the restaurant's life. "Everything here is calculated," explains Lorenzo, who's in charge of the front of house. "I'm slightly OCD when it comes to creating a specific atmosphere; I spend hours on the Remodelista website." The fact that this restaurant could look at home either in Paris or in London is a bonus for the partners: they want the sense of place to be restricted to the plate. Lorenzo likes to say that sixty-five percent of his clientele is international. The unprovincial, sophisticated flair produces an interesting juxtaposition with the cuisine.

Daniele Bendanti used to work at Osteria Bottega, a Bolognese institution, after a period at two-Michelin-starred Arnolfo, in Tuscany, and Lorenzo cut his teeth waiting tables at his family's trattoria, Battibecco. They both grew up with traditional dishes made by their mothers, fathers, and grandmothers. Gradually they became aware of what could be improved. ("Things were often too greasy, an inch of oil over everything: it required heroic digestions.") Many "traditional" restaurants mask their dearth of good ingredients with an overdose of condiments. At Oltre, Bendanti serves a slightly revisited version of Bolognese cuisine, based on quality local products. His version is lighter, and it's got some fun twists. For example, his Roll di Polpettone is based on a staple of the Bolognese household, meatloaf made with leftover tortellini filling. ("Sometimes when making tortellini, some filling is left over. What do you do with it? You roll it up, then bake it in the oven," he explains.) Oltre's version is creamy: a small amount of potato is added to the roll and the polpettone is cooked sous-vide, then topped with Daniele's version of friggione, a sauce made with tomatoes, loads of white onions, salt, and olive oil (replacing lard in the original).

Another signature is Retrosuperfuture Spuma di Mortadella, a desecrating take on mortadella mousse, a classic antipasto from the '70s and '80s, made with cubed (heresy!) mortadella and lemon zest (sacrilegious when added to mortadella), atop a sheep ricotta foam. The dish links back to Massimo Bottura's *Ricordo di un Panino alla Mortadella*, which is concentrated mortadella mousse served with a cube of bread made with pork rinds and pancetta, an homage to the panino con la mortadella the Modenese chef used to eat at home for merenda. (Bottura's book is on display in Oltre's dining room.) "Massimo is a huge source of inspiration: whomever wants to push the envelope in a certain direction inevitably crosses his path," both guys say.

The cuisine at Oltre is not the main reason why I think this is an interesting project. What makes Oltre noteworthy is not the food; rather, it's what you drink with your food. In a country where, for the longest time, no beverages other than water, wine, gazzosa, and grappa were served at restaurants, the membrane is rupturing. It makes for a much more fun experience, more nuanced and complete.

The man behind the bar is Nico Salvatori, a young Modenese well-known among mixology experts. A peek at his station reveals jars full of infusions and fermenting liquids. Personally, I was struck by his ice-carving technique: the monolithic block in my Milano-Torino-Copenhagen (an Italian classic spiked with a very aromatic sparkling tea; page 227) was visually stunning and certainly proved why so many bartenders treat ice as an integral ingredient. And while natural wines are starting to elbow their way in to restaurants across the country, one quirky label at a time, Oltre already carries a selection of 300 of such bottles, curated by Lorenzo.

The bar is a recent addition, designed to pamper guests with a broader dining experience. A drink before dinner, while waiting for a table. A nightcap before leaving. "Cocktail and food pairing is tricky with our style of cuisine, so we recommend pairing distilled spirits instead, like mezcal, which goes well with our fresh rigatoni with Cinta Senese sausage," says Lorenzo. Though if you decide to eat your tortellini with a gin and tonic, nobody will kick you out.

Milano Torino Copenhagen
Milano Torino Copenhagen

Nico Salvatori's recipe calls for "RØD", a sparkling tea developed by sommelier Jacob Kocemba for Copenhagen Sparkling Tea Company, with sparkling wine and ten different types of tea, which are infused at different temperatures and then fermented. Hibiscus is what imparts the dominant note to this concoction: as an alternative, you can use the Sparkling Hibiscus Tea recipe below as a substitute.

Ice cubes
1 oz. Milano-Torino reduction (recipe follows)
1 ½ cups RØD (or substitute Sparkling Hibiscus Tea, recipe follows)
Red berries, for garnish

For 1 cocktail

Fill a Collins glass with ice cubes. Fill about halfway with Sparkling Hibiscus Tea, add the Milano-Torino reduction; top with Sparkling Hibiscus Tea. Garnish with red berries and serve immediately.

Milano-Torino Reduction
½ cup (4.2 oz.) Campari
Scant ½ cup (3.8 oz.) Gagliardo Bitter Radicale (or substitute Luxardo Bitters)
2 ½ teaspoons Gagliardo Bitter Radicale Extra (you may substitute Fernet Branca)
¾ cup (6 oz.) Cinzano Rosso vermouth
1/3 cup (2.5 oz.) Punt & Mes vermouth

Makes about ½ cup

Combine all ingredients in a medium-sized saucepan over medium heat and bring to a boil; cook, stirring occasionally, until mixture has reduced by two thirds. Keep an eye on the pan; the liquid may ignite but it will extinguish itself once the alcohol has evaporated. Once the flame has gone out, boil for another 10 minutes. Remove from heat and let cool at room temperature; the mixture will thicken as it cools.

Sparkling Hibiscus Tea
2 cups boiling water
3 hibiscus tea bags
¼ cup granulated sugar
2 tablespoons freshly squeezed lemon juice
2 cups sparkling rosé wine

For 4 cups of sparkling tea

Combine boiling water and tea bags in a large carafe; cover and set aside to steep for 4 minutes. Remove tea bags and add sugar to hot tea. Stir until sugar dissolves; set aside to cool. When cool, add lemon juice and transfer to refrigerator. When ready to serve, pour in sparkling rosé wine and stir to combine.

PIETRO VERGANO

& ANDREA GHERRA

Something about Turin feels slow, monarchic, and dignified. Whether in San Salvario, an eclectic, rowdy neighborhood near the Porta Nuova train station, or on majestic piazza Vittorio, with its colonnade and the views of river Po and the hills, you will breathe a very particular air. It's the quiet, sometimes torpid pride that comes from having been the home of the royal house of Savoy, the first capital city of the unified reign of Italy, the cradle of so much fine intellectual and literary work, the home of the Fiat and the Agnelli families. Through thick and thin—a shifting political climate, a slow economic recovery, a few factories shuttering, a recent Winter Olympics bid lost to Milan and Cortina d'Ampezzo—it keeps a stiff upper lip.

Walking its streets, one might perceive something else too: the sweet scent of civiltà del bere. Café culture, the rituals of coffee and alcohol, are engrained in Turin's social fabric (just like in Trieste's, another slow, dignified, and piazza-heavy city): Turin is the birthplace of vermouth, and certainly there is a reason why the alleged precursor of the Negroni and Americano cocktails, made with sweet vermouth and Campari, is called Mi-To, from Milano-Torino. The city is surrounded by prime vineyard territory—Langhe and Roero, Barolo, Barbaresco. What better city, then, to explore in search of the "new osteria"? The equivalent of a tavern, a place one would go to drink, and maybe eat a couple of piattini (small plates), the osteria format is as equally important as the trattoria (the two share the same informality, but an osteria is more about drinks and a trattoria more about food) in redefining a new cucina italiana. It is popular, it speaks to the masses. And just like in a trattoria (actually even more), the host (l'oste) is key.

In the center of Turin, near the Palazzo Reale and Teatro Regio, where the narrow streets still follow the original orthogonal grid, amidst sleepy squares, public gardens, and cast-iron lamp posts, there are two such hosts, Pietro Vergano and Andrea Gherra. One blonde and slender, the other dark-haired and muscular. They're friends and business partners, and they run two very well-executed examples of neo-trattoria and neo-osteria: Consorzio and Banco. I present them together, because one couldn't exist without the other, and also because Pietro Vergano is really an oste at heart.

"Andrea used to work in a restaurant; I worked in a wine shop," says Pietro. "We both loved to go out to eat and drink and we dreamt of a place where we could find quality without all the superfluous elements that so often discouraged us from actually choosing a restaurant meal over a home-cooked one." Andrea adds; "Back then you had plenty of restaurants outside of Turin, in the countryside, were you could eat really well, while there were only probably five fairly good places in town, traditional places. The scene was pretty stagnant."

Consorzio was the first of the two to open its doors, and to this date that's where the partners start most of their days, sharing the first of a long series of espressi. Both are finicky about their coffee: they use a Dalla Corte coffee machine and get their coffee from a selected group of roasteries, like Cibbì Specialty Coffee, which source beans that are hand-picked in sustainable mountain plantations, above five thousand feet.

Consorzio's Dalla Corte is where we congregate to have our first chat. It's mid-morning and the restaurant is awakening. Pietro has already gone through bookings and orders, a mound of meat is being browned in the large, old kitchen, waiters are prepping the two dining rooms for service, and the staff meal will be served shortly. The raw-milk cheese fridge hums, the walls glow softly, their terracotta and gray paint layered and chipped, dotted with a few cheeky posters designed by Gianluca Cannizzo, who serves as art director for both restaurants (in Banco's bathroom there's a gigantic nude of a woman, her pubic hair replaced by a bunch of grapes, and featuring the words "naturist wine"). There's a very specific light, a combination of rose-gold and natural. It's homey, though far from stereotypical.

Pietro's brand of hospitality is tough love. He's well aware of it, secretly proud. "It took me a while to figure out what interacting with guests really meant, what it entailed. My biggest flaw is that I'm still too focused on the things I like, everything feels very personal to me." He's quick to check his customers, if he thinks they need it. He's also good at reading people, so he'll know who will hopelessly stick to agnolotti gobbi and fassona beef tartare ("Umph," he says, with a slight eye-roll) and who will instead order marinated trout with vegetables in carpione and sage mayo, or the slightly revisited version of *ravioli di finanziera*, or the house tongue dish, which is served with a horseradish buttermilk sauce instead of the usual salsa verde (page 234). "Our cuisine is traditional, revisited sure, but within reason. Recipes change, but flavors can't: there are specific deep-seated references we must respect, because they define us," says Pietro.

The kitchen at Consorzio was originally run by chef Miro Mattalia and, since his departure, it has been run by his brigade. Together with his staff, Pietro has built a "holy alliance among producers, transformers and conscious customers," focusing on quality ingredients, many of which are Slow Food Presidia. Wine is no exception: it is equally important to Pietro as, say, an heirloom variety of tomato. ("Can you be a maniac about your veggies and your meat and then half-ass it when it comes to wine? I say no!") Pietro attended his first natural wine fair in 2003, the same year he received his sommelier certificate. "Didn't understand a thing!" he laughs. But as his knowledge of natural wine deepened, he became more selective and hardcore. It's an uncompromising approach he shares with his business partner.

EDMONDO AMATI presenta

UGO   MICHEL
MARCELLO   TOGNAZZI PICCOLI   PHILIPPE
MASTROIANNI   NOIRET

LA GRANDE ABBUFFATA

con ANDREA
FERRÉOL   un film di   PANAVISION
                 MARCO FERRERI   EASTMANCOLOR

Andrea and I walk the few meters that separate the two restaurants. Just like at Consorzio, the focus at Banco is on natural wines. Pietro and Andrea collaborated with Piedmontese winery Principiano on a sulfite-free limited edition of their Barolo Serralunga, four hundred bottles that bear the name of Consorzio and are served by the glass at both restaurants. It was quite the big deal: according to Pietro, Piedmont's natural wine scene is still lagging behind other regions. "Piedmont is stuck in its own tradition, that's the problem."

In addition to the house Barolo, both restaurants also carry a Barolo chinato, a rare white chinato (called "Lulì"), and a vermouth, produced originally by Mauro Vergano, Pietro's uncle, and now by Pietro and his cousin. "At Banco you can order a Negroni, an Americano, a gin and tonic. But mostly people come here to drink wine," explains Andrea. "We opened this place because we wanted to play with something even more informal than Consorzio, where people could come all day long to have a good glass and eat something easy and delicious. We don't use tablecloths, our aprons are made of denim. Our first rule is conviviality." (Andrea is a less tough host than Pietro. It doesn't mean he's less attentive. He can be unflinching, but he's naturally jovial.)

What struck me at Banco, the reason why I think it's a great example of neo-osteria, is its cuisine, a cuisine I find exceptionally strong for such a casual place, a result of the same focus on ingredients as Consorzio, paired with an even more pressing need to be inventive and nimble (the lack of storage space leads to daily market supply runs). The kitchen (at the time of my visit the chef in charge was Marco Massaia) is miniscule but it manages to produce some pretty impressive piattini, such as confit potatoes with sea urchin (the potatoes are cooked in clarified beef fat, reserved from the cooking of meats, an example of the restaurant's no-waste policy), a wonderful meat terrine with pistachios and candied fruit, and a phenomenal giardiniera, made with both fruits and vegetables. Right by the entrance of the restaurant (fledged by two tiny cellars, which overlook the street) there's a rotisserie oven where the house famous Sriracha chickens (page 237) are spit roasted for hours.

"I remember going to Paris when bistronomie was exploding: you could eat exceptionally well in some pretty dingy places. Giovanni Passerini's idea of Italian cuisine was another big source of inspiration. We were lucky to be introduced to him while in the French capital." (Barcelona is also a reference, as it often is with bars and restaurants specializing in natural wines.)

The scene has grown since Banco's opening, and many new places have followed in its footsteps, though Andrea is quick to point out Turin is not Milan, and tourism is not a driving force, yet. "The cool thing about Turin is that it's a big city with a small-town mentality and vibe. We're all friends, so if someone opens a cute wine bar with sensible food near me, I'm happy because I have another place to go to."

Interestingly, he says, the newer enoteche and lounges are surpassing the very *caffè storici* that made Turin famous.

"Those used to be the elegant places you would go to for an impeccable Negroni or a Martini. Nowadays it depends: is the head bartender there, do they make their Negroni with plain Campari, do they invest in specialty vermouth? They need to catch up." Hopefully they will. Hell, even Pietro's barber is now serving wine and coffee.

Lingua al Verde
Beef Tongue "al Verde"

The cuisine of Consorzio flirts with tradition in a contemporary yet not overly conceptual way: small tweaks and a solid knowledge of the big book of tradition make for delicious dishes that feel familiar as much as they are subtly surprising. This play on the classic Piedmontese beef tongue is one such dish; the original is served with salsa verde, a sauce made with parsley and an acidic base. Salsa verde is typically served as an accompaniment to bollito misto, together with mostarda di frutta (a classic recipe of candied spicy fruit). In this version, salsa verde is a horseradish sauce spiked with wild garlic oil.

2 carrots, coarsely chopped
2 yellow onions, peeled and coarsely chopped
2 celery stalks, coarsely chopped
2 fresh or dried bay leaves
5 sprigs of thyme
2 sprigs of rosemary
1 beef tongue
4 cups stale bread cubes
3 cups canola oil, for frying
½ cups chopped Italian parsley
Extra-virgin olive oil
Beef glaze (recipe follows)
Buttermilk-Horseradish sauce (recipe follows)
Wild Garlic Oil (recipe follows)
Baby Carrots and Quick-Pickled Shallots (recipe follows)

Serves 4 to 6

Combine carrots, onions, celery, and herbs in a large stockpot. Fill with cold water and bring to a boil over high heat. Gently lower the beef tongue into the water, bring back to a boil then adjust heat to maintain a steady simmer for 3 to 3 ½ hours. The tongue is done when it is very tender: you should be able to easily insert a toothpick or fork into it without any resistance. Lift tongue from broth and discard broth. Peel the tongue while it is still hot; transfer to the refrigerator and let cool completely.

Heat the canola oil in a deep frying pan over high heat. When oil is hot, fry the bread cubes until golden brown and crunchy, about 3 minutes. Transfer fried bread cubes to a paper towel-lined plate to cool. Change paper towels after 10 minutes and allow to cool completely. Combine bread cubes and parsley in a food processor. Pulse until you obtain a crumbly, uniform breadcrumb mixture; set aside.

Preheat oven to 400°F and line a baking sheet with a piece of parchment paper. Remove tongue from refrigerator and slice crosswise into 6 to 8 large portions. Spread the breadcrumb mixture onto a plate.

Heat 2 tablespoons of olive oil in a large frying pan over high heat. Add the tongue and cook, turning occasionally, until golden brown on both sides. Meanwhile, warm the beef glaze and pour into a shallow bowl. Once tongue slices are seared, transfer them one at a time to the bowl, turning to coat thoroughly with the glaze. Place slices on the parchment-lined baking sheet and bake just until heated through, 3 to 4 minutes. Working one at a time, lift a slice of glazed tongue with tongs and dip into the breadcrumb mixture, pressing to coat completely. Repeat with remaining tongue and breadcrumbs.

Meanwhile, heat a tablespoon of olive oil in a small frying pan over medium-high heat. Add baby carrots and sauté briefly until shiny and fragrant. Transfer to a small bowl; season with salt and Wild Garlic Oil to taste.

To serve: place one piece of breaded tongue in the center of each plate. Arrange baby carrots and shallot slices next to the tongue; accompany with Buttermilk-Horseradish sauce and Wild Garlic Oil. Serve warm.

Beef Glaze
8 lbs. beef bones
Extra-virgin olive oil
3 carrots, diced
4 celery stalks, diced
1 yellow onion, peeled and diced
8 ½ cups red wine (about 2 ¾ bottles)

Makes about 2 cups

Preheat oven to 500°F, place beef bones on a baking sheet and roast in hot oven for 30 minutes. Meanwhile, heat a tablespoon of olive oil in a very large stockpot over medium-high heat and add carrots, celery, and onion. Cook, stirring occasionally, until vegetables are tender and onions are translucent, about 7 minutes. Remove bones from oven and carefully transfer them to the stockpot. Pour in the wine and add enough water to just cover the bones. Bring to a boil over high heat; adjust flame to maintain a slow, steady simmer for at least 8 hours, up to 12 hours. Remove and discard bones; filter broth into a small saucepan over medium heat. Bring to a simmer and cook until reduced to a thick yet pourable glaze, 30 minutes to 1 hour.

Wild Garlic Oil
½ cup grapeseed oil
5 cups wild garlic leaves (or ramp leaves), washed and spun dry

Combine the oil and garlic leaves in a blender and process until smooth. Transfer to an airtight jar, close tightly and keep in a dark place overnight. The next day, filter through a fine mesh sieve.

Buttermilk-Horseradish Sauce
2 cups buttermilk
¼ cup finely grated, fresh horseradish root

Makes 2 cups

Combine buttermilk and grated horseradish in a small bowl. Cover tightly and refrigerate for 3 hours. Remove from refrigerator, uncover, and filter with a fine mesh sieve. Discard solids.

Baby Carrots and Quick-Pickled Shallots
1/3 cup plus 2 tablespoons red wine vinegar
¼ cup sugar
2/3 cup water
10 baby carrots, trimmed and scrubbed
2 shallots, peeled and very thinly sliced crosswise
Salt

Serves 4

Combine vinegar, sugar, and water in a small saucepan and bring to a boil over medium-high heat. Place shallots in a heat-proof bowl. When the sugar is dissolved and the mixture is boiling, pour hot liquid over the shallots in the bowl. Set aside to cool completely. Drain, discarding liquid; set aside shallots.

Prepare an ice bath. Bring a small saucepan of water to a boil over high heat. Add 1 teaspoon salt and baby carrots; cook for 3 minutes. Drain carrots and transfer immediately to ice bath; let cool completely. Drain and set aside.

Heat a tablespoon of oil in a small frying pan. Add baby carrots and cook, shaking pan occasionally, until carrots are shiny and tender, about 5 minutes. Combine shallots and carrots, sprinkle with salt, and serve warm.

Pollo allo Spiedo con Sriracha
Sriracha Roast Chicken

This spit-roast can be oven-roasted at home: the key is the marinade which combines both beer and Sriracha for maximum moisture and a complex flavor, full of umami. Leftovers will work well in a sandwich: top them with Damiano's Giardiniera (recipe on page 91) plus a generous drizzle of EVOO or a dollop of the Fooders' Garlic and Chive Mayo (recipe on page 243).

1 whole chicken (about 4 lbs.)
1 tablespoon kosher salt
1 tablespoon smoked paprika
2 tablespoons sriracha
1 (12 oz.) bottle of lager
1 shallot, peeled
4 sprigs of thyme
2 sprigs of rosemary
2 sprigs of sage
2 fresh or dried bay leaves
5-6 whole, dried juniper berries

Special equipment: an instant-read thermometer

Serves 4

Rinse chicken under cold water, pat dry with paper towels and rub generously with kosher salt, inside and out. Stir together smoked paprika, sriracha, and beer. Brush chicken liberally with this mixture, inside and out, and transfer chicken to an airtight container or plastic zipper bag. Pour beer mixture over the chicken and let marinate in the refrigerator for 4 hours or overnight, turning occasionally.

Preheat oven to 425°F. Remove chicken from marinade. Pour leftover marinade into a small saucepan and bring to a boil over medium-high heat. Boil steadily until it has reduced by about 60%, about 20 minutes.

Insert the shallot, fresh herbs, and juniper berries into the chest cavity of the chicken, tuck the wings under (truss if desired) and transfer to a roasting pan. Place chicken in preheated oven and cook for 20 minutes. Remove from oven, baste with pan juices, brush with some of the reduced marinade, and return to oven. Continue cooking, basting with pan juices and brushing with reduced marinade every 20 minutes. The chicken is done when an instant-read thermometer inserted in the thickest part of the thigh reads 165°F, 1 to 1 ½ hours. Remove from oven and let rest for 10 minutes before carving and serving. Stir together remaining pan juices with the reduced marinade and serve warm with the chicken.

THE

FOODERS

We're at the loft of Francesca Barreca and Marco Baccanelli, a/k/a The Fooders, in Rome's San Lorenzo neighborhood, and even though the task at hand—shooting their portrait—should be easy, we've hit a wall.

Marco is standing on a rolling library ladder, showing us some of the many objects (cookbooks, lucha libre masks, action figures, and other assorted knickknacks from their trips all over the world) in their collection, Francesca is standing at the foot of the ladder. I ask her if she would like to hold the ladder for Marco.

"Absolutely not!" she quips. "I don't want people to think I'm his devoted sidekick."

Because the kitchen is the Roman couple's effective habitat, we'll end up shooting them as they prepare the Cotoletta di Broccolo Romanesco (recipe on page 243). Seeing them talk over each other, as their hands move swiftly from prepping the vegetable cutlets to the *genovese di pannicolo* (a sauce made by slow braising lots of onions and skirt steak) they will serve with *ruote* (pasta "wheels"), is like watching an episode of *Mad About You*. It's zinger after zinger, with Francesca interjecting in one of Marco's passionate monologues to ask, "Excuse me, can I say something too," with an eye-roll.

Mazzo, the Fooders' restaurant, closed with a memorable block party in January 2019. With just one communal table seating no more than ten people at a time, it was part of a small group of fun yet substantial restaurants, pizzerie, and bars that helped turn Centocelle, a peripheral, working-class neighborhood, into a gastronomic destination. More than that, it helped define a genre—revisited traditional Roman cuisine—and create a community of customers and chefs who recognized themselves in the couple's approach and coalesced around it.

It closed because Francesca and Marco, who had started out as caterers and interns at high profile restaurants, were feeling the constraints of their space, and because the far-flung community they had contributed to creating inspired them to embark on a nomadic quest. They then launched "Mazzo Invaders," a series of dinners that, over the course of one year, took them from Italy to the rest of Europe and to Japan.

"With Mazzo we had achieved more than we had hoped for," says Francesca, "but we kept interacting with the same group of people over and over. We felt the urge to travel, discover new things and compare experiences. We closed the restaurant and we set out to do not just pop-ups, but also multi-hand dinners and festivals, whatever our friends would throw at us."

"Per cambiare devi soffrì," you must suffer in order to evolve, says Marco.

Evolution doesn't mean tearing apart Mazzo's original concept; traveling and sharing in the traditions of the places they visited taught the couple that what they had been doing was right. ("A Roman culinary DNA is our strength.") What was wrong was the small scale of it. As they gear up to open a new Mazzo, still in Rome, they're thinking of a bigger, multifunctional space, open all day, and alive with a constant flow of colleagues who will come and work alongside them. "Look, when the trattoria was born, it was contemporary, so why shouldn't neo-trattoria be," asks Marco. "Otherwise it's fiction or, worse, folklore."

The Fooders are not necessarily interested in addressing the flavor codes and gestures of Italian cuisine, like Damiano Donati of Fuoco e Materia does (page 82), and they're not approaching tradition through the lens of fine dining, like the brothers from Al Cjasal (page 216). Much like the guys at Oltre (page 222) do with the diehard food habits of Bologna, they stick to what they know best and love most viscerally, Roman tradition, and imbue it with what they have absorbed from the places they've come to love (like St. John's in London). Comfort, precision, informality, and a certain underlying smoothness. "We're like jazz musicians, we improvise based on standards. When you cook pannicolo on the grill, which is what most people do, there's always an end piece that is discarded: we collect all those pieces and make the ragù that goes in our genovese. We serve lamb pluck, or coratella (which traditionally refers to only a few internal organs-heart, lungs and liver-of small animals) on bread, with pecorino cheese and concia, which is the Roman version of a scapece marinade."

Bread comes from Bonci, meat from Roberto Liberati. Mazzo served cocktails (a dry Martini was the recommended pairing with the coratella) and natural wines. Some very Italian ingredients were accented by exotic elements, though it was never "fusion," and it never will be. The five-spice free-range pork belly with parsnip giardiniera and cauliflower, which I never tried, was reportedly finger-licking good. There was braised lettuce with butter and squid sauce, a "fake" version of butter and anchovies—cheaper too.

Where Mazzo used to be, Francesca and Marco have opened Legs, a fast food joint with a fried chicken-centric menu. They're using it as their temporary release valve while they get ready for their next chapter.

"If Mazzo was crushing it," concludes Marco, "Mazzo 2.0 will have to kill it."

Cotoletta di Broccolo Romanesco, Maionese all'Erba Cipollina

Romanesco Cauliflower Cutlets with Garlic and Chive Mayo

Francesca Barreca and Marco Baccanelli use extremely coarse homemade breadcrumbs for extra-crunch, which provide a nice contrast to the soft Romanesco coated in creamy pecorino and egg: the same breadcrumbs (made with Bonci's bread) are also used for the famous fried chicken served at Legs, the street food joint they co-own in Rome's Centocelle. To obtain the same texture at home you can refresh some stale bread in the oven for a few minutes at 200°F and either blitz it in a food processor until coarsely ground, or cover it with a dishcloth and beat it with a rolling pin. The delicious mayonnaise they serve with this vegetarian cotoletta is best made the day before.

1 medium Romanesco cauliflower, about 1¾ lbs.
3 fresh or dried bay leaves
5 dried juniper berries
2 cups homemade, coarse breadcrumbs
1 cup all-purpose flour
4 large eggs
6 oz. aged pecorino cheese, finely grated (you may substitute Parmigiano Reggiano)
6 cups peanut oil, for frying
Garlic and Chive Mayonnaise (recipe follows), for serving

Special Equipment:
Candy Thermometer or Frying Thermometer, optional

Serves 4

Wash and pat dry the cauliflower and remove the outer leaves. Cut the head in half through the core, then into 1-inch wedges through the core. Make sure to keep a bit of the core intact as the "point" of each wedge (that's what will hold it together).

Place a large pot of water over high heat. Add the bay leaves and juniper berries. When the water boils, add a tablespoon of salt and the cauliflower wedges. Boil gently until the core is tender when poked with a toothpick, 5 to 7 minutes. Gently remove from the water with a slotted spoon or spider and let dry on a paper towel-lined dish.

Crack 4 eggs into a wide, shallow bowl; stir with a fork to blend. Finely grate ½ of a clove of garlic and add to the eggs along with the grated pecorino cheese. Whisk vigorously to combine.

Pour the flour and the breadcrumbs into two separate, shallow bowls; stir a pinch of salt into each bowl. Working with one at a time, dip cauliflower wedges into flour, then eggs, and then breadcrumb mixture, pressing to coat. Place breaded wedges on a plate and refrigerate for 30 minutes or until ready to fry. (The wedges can chill in the refrigerator for several hours or overnight.)

Heat the oil in a large skillet or wok to 350°F, or until some

breadcrumbs sizzle immediately when tossed in the hot oil. Carefully lower a couple of the breaded wedges into the hot oil and fry, turning once, until golden brown, 4 to 6 minutes. Transfer to a paper towel-lined plate and sprinkle with salt; repeat with remaining wedges.

Serve cauliflower cutlets warm with Garlic and Chive Mayonnaise .

Garlic and Chive Mayonnaise

1 cup chopped chives
½ peeled garlic clove
1 ½ cup grapeseed oil
5 large egg yolks, cold
½ teaspoon salt, or more to taste
3 tablespoons apple cider vinegar

Makes about 2 ½ cups

Combine chives, ½ of a garlic clove, and 2/3 cup grapeseed oil in a blender. Blend to combine; set aside for 30 minutes to allow flavors to meld.

Filter the chive-infused oil with a fine mesh sieve into a measuring cup, pressing down on the chives with a wooden spoon or spatula to release oil. Place the cold egg yolks in the cup of an immersion blender (or a jar just wider than the head of the immersion blender). Blend until well combined. With the immersion blender running, add the infused oil, a tablespoon at a time, making sure each addition of oil is completely incorporated before adding the next. When the mixture is creamy and emulsified, add 1 teaspoon salt, or more to taste, and 1 tablespoon of vinegar. Blend until well combined. Keep the blender running and add the rest of the grape seed oil in a very slow, steady stream until incorporated. Add the remaining vinegar, a teaspoon at a time, blending thoroughly after each addition. Taste for salt and add more if necessary. Transfer to an airtight container and refrigerate until ready to serve, or up to 2 days.

MARTINA MICCIONE

& CARLA DE GIROLAMO

When Tipografia Alimentare first opened, customers were baffled. They would glance at the Kraft paper roll with the handwritten list of dishes of the day, read things like "beetroot, Ispica's sesame, elderflower, fermented apricot," and beat it. "People literally up and left!" laughs Martina Miccione, the young co-owner. But after a few months, it became one of the most talked-about restaurants in Milan.

Calling it "restaurant," however, is not entirely correct. Martina, her mother and business partner Carla De Girolamo, and chef/forager Mattia Angius, who helped shape Tipografia's culinary philosophy, think of it as a "food hub." A cozy, multi-functional space, open from breakfast until late night; a place to go have good coffee and a slice of cake, to sample plates from the vegetable-driven lunch menu (there is no dinner service, but aperitivo comes with a selection of snacks), to drink natural wine or craft beer (selected by Martina), to meet small producers and buy their products directly, to work, to mingle. This kind of place is already popular in other worldly cities, but not so much in Italy, where the codes of gastronomic experience have historically been less flexible, so that a bar is a bar, a restaurant a restaurant, and mixing them, shaking things up, seemed to be almost unthinkable, until recently.

Both Martina and Mattia are graduates of Slow Food's University, in Pollenzo. After working in Norway and Denmark they returned to Milan to help Martina's mom, a journalist with thirty years' experience who decided to leave her magazine job and make a foray into a new industry. At first the trio considered buying a food truck, but then—because Carla is Pugliese—they thought of opening a place specializing in panzerotti, a sort of small fried calzoni typical of southern Italy. "Then we thought of a bar, because my mom had always had this romantic fantasy of owning a comfortable place where she could talk to people, and get to know them," says Martina. "It couldn't be a specialty coffee shop, because frankly I couldn't picture her explaining things like 'single origin' filter."

One day, while walking along the Naviglio della Martesana, one of Milan's canals, in a part of the city where blue-collar workers and intellectuals mingle, Martina and Mattia had their epiphany. "There were so many people out walking along the canal, it felt safe, happy, familiar." They found a former post office very close to the Naviglio, eighteen hundred square feet with generous light coming in from the street. Only problem: it didn't have an exhaust pipe. "And with that we struck gold. We were forced to build our identity around the fact that we could not produce any smoke or vapor in the kitchen. We use a sous-vide machine and an oven."

TipA (as it's known among regulars) serves mostly vegetables, marinated, fermented, dressed with unusual condiments, like a particularly funky *colatura di alici* (an amber-colored anchovy sauce) mixed with breadcrumbs and used to top a dish of grilled green bell peppers and zucchini (page 249). Every day, there are a couple of animal protein options, like frittata or sheep tartare, and during colder months something hearty and deeply satisfying, like a lasagna or a leek flan au gratin. A snout-to-tail approach is enforced when treating meats; the majority of produce, cheese, and charcuterie are Slow Food Presidia and come from artisanal producers. TipA encourages customers to buy these products directly through communal purchasing groups and regularly hosts gatherings to connect food artisans and potential buyers.

Foraging is also a big part of TipA's menu, thanks to Mattia's regular expeditions to the mountains (Piedmont's Valchiusella and Val Grande, Lombardy's Valtellina and Valsassina) and the hills of Oltrepo Pavese. Frittata comes with a side of wild mesclun made with dandelion, sorrel, watercress, yarrow, acacia flowers, nasturtium, clover, and starwort, bursting with natural spiciness and acidity, with nutty and sweet secondary notes. Acidity is particularly dominant in TipA's vegetarian dishes, which is why they are often recommended for sharing. (This is something Italians are not used to: sharing dishes throughout a meal is different from, say, placing a Pyrex of baked ziti in the middle of the table. I doubt Italians could entirely give up the pleasure of having a full serving of one's own dish—we enjoy food too much to not have proprietary sentiments.)

Clearly TipA works because it combines the community-oriented multifunctionality and the coolness of many smart European cafes and bistros with an all-Italian sense of hospitality. In the house of Martina and Carla, two natural-born hostesses, listening to their banter and catching the glances they exchange, sometimes conspiratorial, sometimes incendiary—is half the fun. It's even nicer to see two generations of women come into their own, dispensing a contemporary, spirited version of Italian nurturing. Though Martina's parents are divorced, her father (also a journalist) pops in regularly. Chefs come to hang out and cleanse their palate with the house vegetables (Diego Rossi of Trippa—page 198—loves the baked carrots topped with Sicilian sumac), grandparents take their grandchildren for cookies and fresh juices, young people love the regular pop-ups by other cool Italian restaurants and bakeries, and the DJ sets that accompany those events. In the end, Carla Girolamo got exactly what she wanted: she talks to people, she gets to know them well.

Zucchine, Peperoni e Colatura di Alici
Zucchini, Bell Peppers, and Anchovy Extract

Colatura di alici is a rich, fermented anchovy sauce from Cetara, Campania (which some have traced back to garum, a fermented fish sauce made with fish entrails, common among the ancient Romans, Greeks, and in the Mediterranean basin). The pungent, amber-colored liquid adds an instant and complex kick of umami to any dish with just a few drops. You can buy colatura di alici at specialty and import stores. If you can't find it, you can still make this recipe; simply chop a few oil-packed anchovies into a paste, and mix them with a teaspoon of their own oil to mimic the savory punch of colatura.

2 cups warm water
Salt
2 large zucchini, sliced into thin strips
10 mint leaves, chopped
Freshly-squeezed lemon juice, to taste
Extra virgin olive oil
2 red or yellow bell peppers
1 teaspoon colatura di alici, or more to taste
¼ cup homemade, coarse breadcrumbs
1 teaspoon finely grated lemon zest

Serves 4

Combine 2 cups warm water and 1 teaspoon salt in a glass measuring cup. Stir until salt dissolves. Place zucchini strips in a plastic or glass container or bowl and pour the salt-water solution over them. Cover and refrigerate for 2 hours. Drain and pat dry zucchini; toss with diced mint, a splash of lemon juice and a drizzle of olive oil.

Meanwhile, heat the broiler to high. Place the whole bell peppers on a parchment-lined baking sheet and broil, turning every few minutes, until peppers are black and blistered all over, 10 to 15 minutes. Transfer hot peppers to a bowl and cover tightly; set aside until cool enough to handle. Peel and discard blistered skin and seeds. Cut cleaned peppers into thin strips. Season peppers with colatura di alici, lemon juice, and olive oil to taste.

Heat a medium skillet over medium-high heat. Add a teaspoon of olive oil and breadcrumbs; toast, stirring often, until fragrant and golden, about 5 minutes. Transfer breadcrumbs to a bowl; add lemon zest and salt to taste.

Arrange peppers on a serving dish with marinated zucchini on top; sprinkle with breadcrumb mixture and serve.

FINALE

(ON COMFORT)

Many months ago, I waited tables at Trippa, in Milan, for a memorable multi-chef dinner that brought together many of the subjects of this book. I was already planning my long research journey, and I remember looking at the guys cracking jokes and peering over each other's shoulders with admiration, thinking I had put my finger on something real. "This is a movement," I told myself. I couldn't wait to explore it.

As an Italian in love with my country and culture, I found this discovery to be very comforting. The movement is surely imperfect (you will still find chefs who tell you contemporary Italian cuisine is lacking, that there's nothing interesting happening), but I believe something powerful indeed is stirring and I hope our institutions will do a better job supporting the women and men of the new cucina italiana, creating better platforms (and infrastructures) to foster their discovery.

Indeed, between Bottura's high-wire creations and a plate of amatriciana there's a whole world to be discovered. Sure, you can keep coming to eat amatriciana, if that's your idea of comfort. But consider also this: the movement I described is carrying one of the world's most storied cuisines to its next chapter—not trying to antagonize it, vilify it, or minimize its significance. These young talents are still a product of what (and who) has come before them.

Food can be transformative in so many ways. Its cultural significance is staggering, it's one of the most efficient, universally understood ways of communicating the spirit and values of a given place and time. The women and men of the new cucina italiana are making us Italians more aware not just of our own culinary legacy but also of what we would like to eat now. Their incredible attention to the experience of the meal, to the well-being and happiness of their guests, and to the way their work influences the world around them is making all of us proud. Come meet them.

RESTAURANTS

BY REGION

PIEMONTE
Banco/Consorzio – Andrea Gherra, Pietro Vergano
Reis Cibo Libero di Montagna – Juri Chiotti

LOMBARDIA
Cascina Lagoscuro – Luca Grasselli
Erba Brusca – Alice Delcourt
Lido 84 – Riccardo Camanini
Materia – Davide Caranchini
Il Portico – Paolo Lopriore
Tipografia Alimentare – Martina Miccione, Carla De Girolamo
Trippa – Diego Rossi

VENETO
Al Cjasal – Mattia and Stefano Manias

FRIULI-VENEZIA GIULIA
L'Argine a Vencò – Antonia Klugmann

EMIGLIA-ROMAGNA
DaGorini – Gianluca Gorini
Oltre – Daniele Bendanti, Lorenzo Costa

TOSCANA
Fuoco e Materia – Damiano Donati
Ristorante Giglio – Benedetto Rullo, Lorenzo Stefanini, Stefano Terigi

LAZIO
Retrobottega – Giuseppe Lo Iudice and Alessandro Miocchi
Marzapane – Francesco Capuzzo Dolcetta
The Fooders – Marco Baccanelli, Francesca Barreca

CAMPANIA
Pepe in Grani – Franco Pepe
Concettina ai Tre Santi – Ciro Oliva

ABRUZZO
Reale – Niko Romito
Tosto – Gianni Dezio

PUGLIA
Bros' – Floriano Pellegrino, Isabella Potì
Mezza Pagnotta – Francesco and Vincenzo Montaruli

ACKNOWLEDGMENTS

This book wouldn't exist had it not been for a fortuitous encounter with Caitlin Leffel, on one hot Milanese summer night, during Expo 2015. Little did I know this razor sharp American editor, who is also a marathon runner obsessed with typography and small batch breweries, who could talk anybody under the table and crush all negativity with her unyielding optimism, would years later become the biggest champion of this project and guide me with her soothing patience and wit. I will forever be grateful to that tornado of energy. Today I am lucky to call her friend.

I share this adventure with two more key people who are now part of my extended family: Alberto Blasetti and Laurel Evans, my photographer and food editor. Their commitment to *The New Cucina Italiana* has been monumental and I was inspired by the passionate stubbornness they have faced each challenge with.

Alberto has driven hundreds of kilometers, shot miles of film (wait, we don't have that anymore), changed flat tires, lied down on interstates, climbed on top of bookshelves—all for the sake of a good shot. I have yet to meet a photographer more capable of economizing time and space, without compromising the quality of his work (or his sense of humour). He's also a profound connoisseur of the world of restaurants and gastronomy, something not necessarily associated with the job description of a food photographer. His insight has come to my aid on more than one occasion while producing this book.

And Laurel, well, what can I say about this dynamite of a girl? Ask her about that time she tested five recipes at the same time on her miniature workhorse of a stovetop. Or about that time she tried to get her kids, Juanita and Attilio, to like the pucker-up acidic "giardiniera." She hails from Texas but has been living in Italy for many years with her husband Emilio and was very helpful in dealing with conversions, substitutions, and all the countless, sometimes subtle adaptations that go into transposing recipes—and the language of food—from one culture to the other.

Caitlin, Alberto, and Laurel are people I would happily be marooned on an island with. No joke.

I am grateful to Gio "Tony" Chiappetta for meeting me in Milan, for a day of book browsing (and tripe-eating), and for loving typeface design as much as Caitlin and I do. And Laurel and I owe much to Anna Kovel as well: Anna and I crossed paths like two ships in the night as she was living in Rome yet getting ready to move back to the U.S. She has lent a very helpful extra set of experienced eyes to our recipes.

Finally, there is one more string of my heart that needs to be pulled and struck. While this project was born out of a season of optimism and global appreciation, it wrapped up at a time of deep uncertainty, when essentially the fate of Italy's (and the world's) hospitality and restaurant industry seems to be hanging by a thread. I hope that by the time you read these words, our chefs will be back with a vengeance. I love them fiercely.

First published in the United States of America in 2020 by
Rizzoli International Publications, Inc.
300 Park Avenue South
New York, NY 10010
www.rizzoliusa.com

Copyright © 2021 Laura Lazzaroni
Photography by Alberto Blasetti
Recipe testing by Laurel Evans

Art Direction: Gio Chiappetta
Design: Gio Chiappetta, Bredna Lago

Publisher: Charles Miers
Editor: Caitlin Leffel
Production Manager: Kaija Markoe

Printed in China
2021 2022 2023 2024 / 10 9 8 7 6 5 4 3 2 1
ISBN: 978-0-8478-6855-1
Library of Congress Control Number: 2020935609

Visit us online:
Facebook.com/RizzoliNewYork
Twitter: @Rizzoli_Books
Instagram.com/RizzoliBooks
Pinterest.com/RizzoliBooks
Youtube.com/user/RizzoliNY
Issuu.com/Rizzoli